WIPED

The Curious History of Toilet Paper

by Ronald H. Blumer

To my daughter (who, try as I might, I cannot seem to embarrass anymore.)

Published by:

M_mP

Middlemarch Media Press
2211 Broadway, Suite 2dn
New York, NY 10024
rhblumer@panix.com

Cover illustration *Milord Plumpudding* by Aaron Martinet, 1814

ISBN-13: 978-1489573865

ISBN-10: 1489573860

Copyright © 2013 Middlemarch Media Press

The text of this document has been registered with the Library of Congress TXu001791174

bw1.9

The Muses Recreation

Galen's old rules could not suffice,
Nor yet Hippocrates the wise.
Not teaching, how to dance, can do,
Themselves must come and wipe it too.

Here did lie Virgil, there lay Horace,
Which newly had wiped his, or her arse.
Anacreon reeled too and fro,
Vexed, that they used his papers so.

Here lies the letter of a lover,
Which piecemeal did the thing discover.
Sonnets half written would not stay,
But must necessity obey.

But then the pity to behold
Those ancient authors, which of old
Wrote down for us, philosophy,
Physick, music, and poetry,
Now to no other purpose tend,
But to defend the fingers end.

Sir John Mennes (1599 -1671)
& James Smith (1605 -1667)

TABLE OF CONTENTS

FOREWORD ……………..……………….5
1) SHAME ……………………………..11
2) THE PAST STANK ………………….....30
3) A REFRESHER ON TOILETS ………….51
4) BEFORE PAPER …………………….....79
5) PAPER! …………………………......105
6) ON A ROLL ……………………..….126
7) SELLING IT ……………………….151
8) WATER …………………………….165
9) THE BOTTOM LINE ………………..179
10) TP STATS & FOLLIES ………………186
ENDPAPER ……………………….....196
ABOUT THE AUTHOR ……………..….201
INTERNET SITES ……………………..202
BIBLIOGRAPHY ……..………………..203

FOREWORD

THE AUTHOR ON HIS MUSE

As it has to many, the inspiration for writing a book came to me while I was sitting on the toilet. But not just any toilet. My wife and I were visiting Ephesus, the great port of the ancient Greek and Roman civilization located in present-day Turkey. Ephesus also was a stopping place for Saint Paul the apostle and perhaps the Virgin Mary, and the city where part of the New Testament was written. The toilet in question was in a 2000 year-old communal lavatory built by the Romans, conveniently located across from the city's brothel and up the street from the Library of Celsius, one of the greatest storehouses of knowledge of the ancient world.

Our guide invited our group to sit on some of these accommodations and then, in broken English and even more broken Japanese, lectured us on the wonders and niceties of Roman public lavatories. He described the running water under these facilities, the perfumed air, and the fountain in the center of the room. Musicians entertained the customers. It was a warm and friendly meeting place where citizens of Ephesus did their business while debating politics, philosophy, and the price of wine. The seats of this accommodation were made of marble, and the guide informed us that the patrons first would have one of their slaves sit on the spot to warm up the seat so their wealthy rear ends would not have to endure the shock of cold stone. Nice touch, I thought. The other thought I had (but was too shy to ask) was, "How in an age long before paper, did they—um—wipe their patrician asses?" I determined to look it up at our present-day Celsius library, the repository of all human knowledge—Google—the moment I could get to an Ephesian Internet café.

If you type 'ass wiping - history' as a search term into Google you get millions of hits including many nasty sex sites but not much useful information. One site, 'discussanything.com,' has more questions than answers and sent me to advertisements for hemorrhoid creams—thank you, Google. Another site, proving that there is absolutely everything on the internet, is called The Toilet Paper Museum. It turns out to be not a brick and mortar place but a virtual cyberspace entity created by a music group. The more I searched, the more sites I found dealing with the subject. The problem was that they all seemed to be copying the same superficial information over and over again, and much of this information was obviously wrong.

With the Internet having failed me, and now home from my Turkish toilet musings, I was determined to get to the bottom of this subject (all future puns unintended) by committing, in this wired age, what might be considered a last act of desperation. I decided to go to a book library.

Like Ephesus, New York City has a wonderful research library located on Fifth Avenue, also near one of the city's rare public lavatories (and I'm sure a few brothels that I wouldn't know about). This Celsius is guarded by two imposing stone lions and has marble halls, and frescoed ceilings, and its bowels contain millions of original manuscripts, books, and periodicals. Rummaging through the library's computerized catalogue, I came upon books and articles on toilets, water closets, middens, and privies, but I could not figure out a way of pulling from the library's wealth of information the specific object of my curiosity.

What I needed was a 'subject heading keyword,' and there under the frescoed ceiling, beckoning me with a smiling face, was the friendly research librarian. I am a shy fellow and it took me some time to summon up the courage to approach the marble counter and ask in a quavering voice for the keyword that would unlock the secrets of ass wiping through the ages. The librarian, who I am sure will be regaling future dinner guests with, 'you aren't going to believe this one!', accepted my unusual request with the dispassionate professionalism of a doctor or a priest and attempted to help me. Not only were there no books or papers on the subject, she informed me, the subject itself did not seem to exist. "Well," said I, "just give me the listing of all the books on toilet paper." I was hoping that in their introductions they would touch on pre-toilet paper history. "There aren't any," said the librarian, by now becoming a bit puzzled herself. "Okay, then," said I, "not on the history of toilet paper," just any book on the manufacturing and marketing of toilet paper, it's a multi-billion dollar industry. There must be…" She interrupted me: "Yes our library on Science and Industry is down the street but they too show no books at all having as their main subject, 'toilet paper'. None!"

A chill went down my back. With the myriad of PhD students combing the world for original topics no matter how obscure, with the thousands of authors and journalists scratching out a living trying to write about something new, with the millions of bloggers and tweeters expounding at length on every aspect of human existence, did they all miss this one staring them right in the face every morning? Could it be that I—humble I—had hit on a really fresh subject, one that had never been rigorously investigated in print? Was this like the region labeled 'terra incognita' on antique maps? Would I be the first human to explore this unknown territory? I resolved to take the challenge—to become the Columbus of butt cleaning.

What began as idle curiosity and, yes, a bit of a joke, has led me on a fascinating journey strewn with amazing facts and an odd, crescent-moon-shaped window on the past.

It also turned out to be among the hardest research I have ever done in a life of doing research, because not only are there very few written records about this most mundane of human activities—the raw material for historians—but there seems to be an active avoidance of the subject. And then there was the search-term problem. What should I look for in the indexes or in periodical searches? The subject seems so forbidden that even the search terms are euphemisms of euphemisms: personal hygiene, elimination behavior, toilet etiquette, privies, close-stools, water closets, sanitary tissue.

Books of fiction were no help. It should not surprise the reader to learn that ass wiping (with one jaw-dropping exception) was not the subject of great literature. It is rarely mentioned in diaries and personal histories. Poets and song writers do not rhapsodize its delights. (But I did discover, to my surprise, that it is the subject of religious edicts.)

It seems that the whole subject of defecation has been largely ignored by academics. Perhaps the professional historians, sociologists, and anthropologists of the world suspected that writing about how we poop is not the surest road to tenure. My bookshelves groan with a twenty-four volume set of the Encyclopedia Britannica, but you will not find toilet paper in its 646 page index. The extensive and magnificently illustrated French series A History of Private Life is certainly not squeamish. It details sexual practices, masturbation, torture and death by disemboweling, but barely touches on latrines and contains not a word about toilet rituals throughout history—although this was obviously a significant aspect of private life. You will not find the subject discussed in any broad sweep history book although anal matters certainly did affect the rise and fall of civilizations. Hitler, Napoleon, and Chairman Mao all had rectal problems so severe that they occasionally interrupted their murderous careers. In 480 BCE, Xerxes' Persian army of 800,000 conquered the Greeks but was brought down by dysentery, a disease spread by fecal contamination. Xerxes ultimately lost the war and we will never know how the history of the Western World would be different if the Persians had altered their bathroom habits. In 1414, the English beat the French at the Battle of Agincourt, but half of their longbow archers, suffering from diarrhea, had to fight the war naked from the waist down. Future generals would have to learn and relearn an uncomfortable fact: it is very difficult for man to focus on slaughtering his fellow man while he has the runs.

In my research, I was confounded by many mysteries. Who can explain, for example, why the website titled *The San Diego Area Accountants Guide* had an excellently researched essay (since removed) on the history of toilet paper? Why did an early print advertisement for toilet paper appear in the University of Chicago's scholarly publication *The American Journal of Semitic Languages and Literatures*? Why does the question of the proper orientation of the toilet roll—over or under—cause continually heated debates? I did, however, uncover the surprising fact that

Queen Elizabeth II does not wipe like you or I, as well as a description of Queen Elizabeth I's extraordinary anal cleaning routine. Stay tuned.

All research takes us to new and unexpected worlds and this journey of discovery took me into the darkest and strangest crevices of the human soul. How else would I ever have the occasion to read with delight such publications as Ralph A. Lewin's magnificent dissertation on shit Merde: Excursions in Scientific, Cultural, and Sociohistorical Coprology, David Eveleigh's Privies and Water Closets, with many beautiful full-color illustrations? Then there is the only-in-England academic discipline of cloacopapyrology, in which 'analytical cloaco-papyrologists' conduct learned discussions about the font variations in their collections of imprinted toilet paper.

I've always believed the cliché that truth is stranger than fiction, and over and over again while researching this book, I have thought to myself, 'You can't make this stuff up!' I have tried to document and verify every unbelievable fact and story that appears in the following pages, all the while shaking my head at the strangeness of our particular species of primate.

It also led me into that most fascinating aspect of history, how kings and queens, peasants, soldiers, and priests actually lived their daily lives. It provided a peek into their homes, their routines, and even their intimate fears and hopes. What I learned in the end is that even from this distasteful and ignored activity, performed daily, everywhere by everyone since the beginning of time, we can gain insights into the human condition.

Hold your nose if you must, but read on.

SHAME

Inter urinas et faeces nascimur.
(We are born between urine and feces.)
St Augustine

To understand why it was so difficult to research this topic, I began by imagining a Martian sociologist coming to earth on a fact-finding trip. With interplanetary objectivity he, she, or it would notice a massive quantity of literature, TV programs, blogs, and daily conversations about eating but almost nothing about defecation. To this puzzled researcher, human beings would seem to be violating one of the fundamental laws of physics—all input and no output. Probing deeper, this investigator would discover that, as the song might put it, "The Greeks do it; the Swedes do it; why, even Britishers in tweeds do it." Though we all do it, we just can't bring ourselves to talk about it. As an expert linguist, this Martian researcher would find proof of this fact in our very language.

Language conveys meaning but it also conveys the attitudes and mores of its particular culture. There is no better example of our squeamishness about this subject, than when the English language tries to deal with the subject of human defecation. Instead of saying the word for this most common of human activities, we rely instead on dictionary pages of euphemisms, some naughty and some nice. We have dozens of highly specialized terms to neutralize our emotion or embarrassment about the subject. Doctors refer to stool, feces, or a bowel movement. Scientist and archeologists analyze coprolites and scat, whereas agricultural researchers study excrement under the names night soil or biomass. Since we must discuss this subject with young children, we have developed workarounds with such cute words as poopy, doody, ka-ka, and so forth. For the mathematically inclined, there is the making of 'number two'. Similar euphemisms exist in all languages. Writing about the 'policing of the French language' the author Dominique Laporte remarks that, "when written, shit does not smell. But to ensure that readers are spared all trace of odor, language must first purge itself of a certain lingering stink."[1]

When it comes to the act itself, we are wonderfully creative at avoiding the verb, grabbing onto whatever word or phrase is the most epistemologically distant from the actual act. When King Saul had to answer the call of nature, the Old Testament tells us that he went into a cave to "cover his feet". When pay toilets were installed in England, the act of shitting became 'to spend a penny.' The Chinese under Mao would say they are going to 'the hall of brotherhood'. The French go directly to the shame of the act using the wonderful descriptive expression that a person's honor is under pressure (*être pressé de son honneur*) if they really have to pee or shit. In the days of outhouses, people would say that they are going into the backyard 'to pluck a rose'. To this day, women will excuse themselves to 'powder their noses'. My favorite comes from America's Founding Fathers. When the First Congress met in New York City in 1789, a man was exhibiting a camel and it became quite an attraction. Whenever Madison, Washington or any other august founder had to 'leave the room,' he would whisper to a fellow delegate, "I think I'll go out and take a peep at the camel."[2]

Nothing better epitomizes the shame we all have about our need to shit than the incident reported in Truman Capote's *In Cold Blood*. Perry Smith is about to be hanged. Asked for his final wish he said that he wanted to go the bathroom and empty his bowels because he knew that hanging often resulted in involuntary defecation. This man had brutally slaughtered an innocent family of four, yet his greatest shame was that the undertaker might see that he had crapped in his pants.

When it comes to the subject of places where said number two is deposited, euphemisms build on euphemisms until backwards reels the mind. Frank Muir in his *Social History of the Bathroom* marveled at the fact that we do not have a word in the English language for the 'it' into which we defecate that indicates its actual function. "For something like four thousand years this place where every man and woman alive 'went' once or more every day had never, in any Western language, been given a simple straightforward name."[3] Even the word 'toilet,' as we shall see below and in a later chapter, was invented to disguise its real purpose. The French, normally reluctant to use English words, commonly call it a '*vey say*' from the English WC, for water closet, the Russians call it a туалет pronounced toalet and in Turkish it is a tuvalet.

Even non-Western languages copy English euphemisms. In Bengali this word, বাথরুম, is pronounced, baat room. The Japanese talk about going to the *otearai* (お手洗い), the hand washing sink, or the *keshōshitsu* (化粧室), the powder room. Indeed, the Japanese hide everything to do with defecation practices, quoting the well known proverb also frequently used in political discussions: 臭い物に蓋をする (Keep a lid on stinky things). Filipinos go to the banyo, the Chinese to the *mao kun*, the straw hole. It seems as if no language in the world has a word for the object that clearly describes its function as a shit receptacle. And then there is the hiding of this hiding in a phenomenon that linguists call the euphemistic treadmill. When these non-descriptive words become too commonplace, they themselves become unmentionable, to be replaced with words to avoid the older words. The process is satirized in a Dr. Seuss story when a young boy puts up his hand in class and asks permission to go to the euphemism.

The word 'toilet' started life innocently enough as *'toile'*, French for cloth, specifically the cloth that was draped over a gentleman or lady while his or her hair was being powdered and dressed. Subsequently, it became associated with a lady's dressing table where personal grooming took place; then it became a room where one could wash up; and only in the early twentieth century, primarily in the United States, did the word come to embody the locus of our defecation. In England it is still a 'WC,' short for water closet. And long before that porcelain thing that flushes, when our ancestors did it in pots or in a hole in the ground, they had their own list of euphemisms for the place or thing where the unmentionable was done. A wonderfully learned word comes from medieval abbeys, the 'necessarium,' which in the 18th century became 'the necessary'. The word 'privy' comes from old French meaning 'private,' which is telling in itself, reflecting a profound change in cultural attitudes to bodily functions because, in earlier times, the act of defecation often was anything but private. Throughout the history of the English language we find dictionary pages of words for the thing or place: lavatory (suggesting cleaning not shitting), rest room (suggesting a place where one might take a nap), house of easement, jake, library, loo, the bog-house, a closet (meaning a small room of any kind); the valve closet, the water closet, W.C. (or in French 'le double', for 'double vey', their word for W), comfort stations, powder rooms, house of office, dilberry creek, and so forth. And it wasn't just the word that was taboo. Until very recently, Federal regulations prohibited the showing of even an image of a toilet in an ad on Canadian television.[4] Whatever we called it, or refused to call it throughout history, it was and remains 'the necessary'.

14

> *I do not like this place at all*
> *The seat's too high and the hole's too small*
> *You lay yourself open to the obvious retort,*
> *Your bottom's too big and your legs are too short.*
>
> British bathroom graffiti

In the same way that excretion and toilets could not be talked or written about, toilet paper and the act of rectal cleaning also were unmentionable—if possible, even more taboo. As we shall see, this delicacy became a real problem for advertisers trying to market anal wiping or washing products. With a few exceptions, butt cleaning is not represented in even the most risqué literature or art. Even Hollywood, which delights in shocking and disgusting us with every possible mutilation or oozing of the human body, almost never showed ass wiping and only used descriptions of the act in dialogue as a nasty epithet.[5]

Why all this shame? We talk, write, make movies, and dream about sex, the physical act of which, observed objectively, is not all that pretty. We are not embarrassed by walking, running, sweating, drinking, breathing, sneezing, or sleeping, but all excremental subjects are banned from polite company. Why should this be? If you believe in the lasting influence of early childhood experience, defecation should be a matter of great satisfaction. I know this from my own family history: one of my brothers as a three-year-old was so proud of his excretory accomplishment that he spread the results on the wall of a motel room. Parents highly praise the act, provided that everything happens in the right place and at the right time.

To say that excrement has a bad odor and an unpleasant color may seem to be a universal truth but it would not be obvious to our mythical Martian. This objective observer might point out that many cheeses really stink and that we are surrounded with many brown objects in our world that do not evoke disgust. One school of thought states that defecation is an insult to human pride. Our dreams, our soaring ambitions, our belief that we are not in our essence corporeal beings but spiritual entities is brought to ground every time we are forced to do the necessary. This fact was best expressed by Jonathan Edwards (1703-1758), a leader of early American Protestantism:

> The insides of the body of man is full of filthiness, they contain his bowels that are full of dung, which represents the corruption and filthiness that the heart of man is naturally full of.

And that most Puritan of Puritans, the Massachusetts theologian Cotton Mather vividly expressed a similar idea. His lament about the depravity of the body was triggered by his encounter with a dog:

> I was once emptying the cistern of nature, and making water at the wall. At the same time, there came a dog, who did so too, before me. Thought I, "What mean and vile things are the children of men, in this mortal state! How much do our natural necessities abase us and place us in some regard, on the level with the very dogs!"...Accordingly, I resolved, that it should be my ordinary practice, whenever I stop to answer the one or other necessity of nature, to make it an opportunity of shaping in my mind some noble, divine thought.

Compared to the Victorians, the Puritans were wild party animals. Puritans admitted to enjoying sex and even allowed trial marriages. The prudery of the Victorians, by contrast, knew no bounds. They would comb earlier literature for anything that could possibly offend and censor (bowdlerize) it. Even a reference to a female leg was considered too shocking to appear in print unless it happened to be a leg of mutton. Discussion of human elimination was beyond the unspeakable. Victoria Kelley discovered this while doing research for her book, *Soap and Water*: "Reticence of contemporary sources," she wrote, "betrays a delicacy about what could and couldn't be discussed, rather than concern about over-flowing middens or the cleaning of chamber pots. Books and magazines on child-rearing deal in wearying detail with every aspect of keeping a baby clean, but rarely mention dirty diapers or potty training."

When we look at the past, we tend to look at the immediate past, and so we assume that people always were prudish. In truth, the Victorians with their repression of anything body and bawdy were the exception. Most cultures have had a much more open attitude to affairs of the flesh. But excretion, throughout history, has remained a special case. Although Greeks and Romans freely pooped communally, the act itself was a subject of their bathroom humor and humor is an indication of embarrassment. You will find plenty of scatological humor in Greek comedies, as well as Roman poetry, Chaucer, Shakespeare, Jonathan Swift, and (it would seem) in every culture of the world. It is telling that toilet jokes always have been the lowest of the low—the ultimate expression of vulgarity. And so it remains today. In his book on Greek comedy, Jeffrey Henderson explains:

> Defecatory jokes and routines are the purest kind of obscene comedy, in that a normally hidden aspect of a comic figure's life can be observed and enjoyed publicly. Defecation is indeed one aspect of our lives that must always be hidden (unlike sex), and must always be thought inappropriate in any social context. Sexual jokes can rarely be reduced to such a low level because sex is so important and so complex a part of our lives; defecation is a remarkably uncomplex process.[6]

Henderson describes the fact that the victims of these jokes in Greek comedy were rustics, vulgar characters or foreigners, easy prey as the butt of butt jokes. However expressed, toilet humor is a vivid demonstration that defecation was and remains a subject of shame and repression. Throughout history, toilet humor has had its ups and downs in literature and in art, but the era right before its total suppression in Victorian times may be considered the golden age of shit, piss and farting humor. It is vividly, and even to our jaded eyes, shockingly, brought to life in the widely circulated prints and drawings of the ribald 18th century.[7]

In this 1726 etching by the great William Hogarth, we have an illustration of Gulliver being punished by the Lilliputians by receiving an extreme enema. It originally was intended to be the frontispiece for the first volume of Swift's *Gulliver's Travels*. The editors wisely decided to omit it.

Gillray's view of two party government

For religious leaders, however, the business of defecation was no joking matter. As we shall see in further chapters, their different attitudes to evacuation will have a direct bearing on the subject at hand. Both the Jewish and Muslim religions have strict biblical guidelines in matters of toilet etiquette stressing a general concern for spiritual as well as bodily purity. In an era long before the awareness of germs, these religions recognized the life and death consequences of defecatory cleanliness.

All Western religions considered shit something impure, but not necessarily the act of shitting. The Jewish religion's approach to defecation, for example, is in sharp contrast to the attitudes of the Puritans. Every Orthodox Jewish male is expected to recite a very beautiful ancient blessing—the Asher Yatzar—after relieving himself. The rhythm and poetry of this prayer is lost in translation but the meaning shines through:

Blessed are thou our God King of the Universe who formed human beings with wisdom and created within him many, holes, perforations, hollows and empty spaces. It is known before your throne of glory that if one of these that should be opened is closed, it would not be possible to survive and stand before your presence. Blessed art thou, Oh Lord who forms and healeth all flesh.

בָּרוּךְ אַתָּה ה' אֱלֹהֵינוּ מֶלֶךְ הָעוֹלָם, אֲשֶׁר יָצַר אֶת הָאָדָם בְּחָכְמָה, וּבָרָא בוֹ נְקָבִים נְקָבִים, חֲלוּלִים חֲלוּלִים. גָּלוּי וְיָדוּעַ לִפְנֵי כִסֵּא כְבוֹדֶךָ שֶׁאִם יִפָּתֵחַ אֶחָד מֵהֶם, אוֹ יִסָּתֵם אֶחָד מֵהֶם, אִי אֶפְשַׁר לְהִתְקַיֵּם וְלַעֲמוֹד לְפָנֶיךָ. בָּרוּךְ אַתָּה ה', רוֹפֵא כָל בָּשָׂר וּמַפְלִיא לַעֲשׂוֹת.

No longer "do our natural necessities abase us". Instead, with this prayer, we are reminded to be grateful for the miracle of normal bodily functions. Also implied however, is a telling Jewish vision of an all-powerful God who can keep our holes open, but also has the power to (God forbid) close them.

Similarly, the most ancient teaching of Buddhism stresses the naturalness and the necessity of elimination. This passage is from the rulebook for monks and nuns, the 'Vinaya Pitaka,' whose teachings are thought to date back to 400 BCE:

> Uccara passavakamme: In defecating and in urinating: When the time is come, when the time is proper, if one does not defecate or urinate, then, one's body perspires, one's eyes reel, one's mind is not collected, and illness in the form of sharp pain, fistula, and so forth can arise. But to one who defecates and urinates at the proper time, none of these discomforts, disadvantages, troubles and illnesses shall arise. This is the sense in which this matter should be understood, and in this sense a clear comprehension of purpose in defecation and urination should be taken.

The act is part of their Buddhist view of life with its endless cycle of birth and rebirth. Defecation is an inevitable part of the natural order of things, or to put the following text into modern phraseology: 'shit happens'.

> There is no doer of the act of defecation or urination... Just as from an overfull pitcher water comes out without any desire for coming out, so too, the feces and urine accumulated in the abdomen and the bladder are pressed out by the force of the process of oscillation. Thus the feces and urine coming out thus is neither that bhikkhu's [the ordained monk's] own nor another's. It is just bodily excretion. When from a water-vessel or calabash a person throws out the old water, the water thrown out is neither his nor that of others. It simply forms parts of a process of cleansing. In the form of reflection proceeding in this way clear comprehension of non-delusion should be understood.

There seems to have been an exception for this non-ownership of feces in the practice of Tibetan Buddhism. In former times, the excrement of the Dalai Lama, Tibet's living God, was thought to have magical healing powers. This holy shit was dried and put in amulets, used as a medicine and even as condiment to be sprinkled on food. The Surgeon General of the United States, Dr. W.M. Mew, analyzed a sample of the Grand Lama's poop in a government laboratory to detect its supernatural powers. (As I said in the introduction to this survey, you just can't make this stuff up.) In a report dated April 18, 1889, he concluded that "the ordure" shows evidence that the Lama "had been feeding on a farinaceous" (i.e. starchy) diet" but otherwise it was unremarkable.[8]

Today, although we like to think that we live in a more permissive age, we still cannot bring ourselves to accept matters of defecation in the holistic spirit of these ancient religions. Far from a blessing, it is the subject of both low humor and high art.

The Museum of Contemporary Art in Milan, Italy prominently displays this work by the well known avant-guard artist Piero Manzoni.

Merda d'artista, 1961

"Manzoni went so far as to make his own body, including its excrement, a creative instrument for producing signs and traces to be used in art. In the consumer climate of the postwar boom years, he offered it as a new product to be launched on the market, adapting it to mass production while also playing, not without irony, on the concealment of the object by packaging." [9]

The cans were numbered 1 to 90 and, although priced by their weight in gold, they were eagerly snapped up by museums and collectors. Unfortunately Piero Manzoni's technology was not up to his artistry and the cans are now all leaking at the seams. Some have even exploded—adding to both the conceptual irony and the market value of his oeuvre.

> I am dumbfounded by how little philosophical and metaphysical importance the human mind has attached to the capital subject of excrement.
>
> Salvador Dali

In *The Geography of the House,* W.H. Auden makes this link between poop and art a universal truth:

> *Rodin was no fool*
> *When he cast his Thinker,*
> *Cogitating deeply*
> *Crouched in the position*
> *Of a man at stool.*
>
> *All the arts derive from*
> *This ur-act of making,*
> *Private to the artist:*
> *Makers' lives are spent*
> *Striving in their chosen*
> *Medium to produce a*
> *   De-narcissus-ized*
> *Enduring excrement.*

Both humor and art can illuminate our most unconscious fears, so it is no surprise that psychoanalysts too are very interested in all things anal. According to Sigmund Freud:

> In infancy there is as yet no trace of shame about the excretory functions or disgust at excreta... Children are, indeed, proud of their own excretions and make use of them to help in asserting themselves against adults. Under the influence of its upbringing, the child's coprophilic instincts and inclinations gradually succumb to repression. It learns to keep them secret, to be ashamed of them and to feel disgust at their objects."[10]

Freud's ideas, however, are culturally biased because of the extreme form of toilet training practiced in the Austria of his youth. At five months, long before infants are physically capable of controlling their bowels, they were placed on potties and urged with threats and rewards to give a present to mommy. This Teutonic regimen may have saved on diaper washing but it also imprinted on both patients and their analysts a life-long obsession with affairs of the rear. Looking at the bigger picture, Freud and other thinkers suggested that this learned act of defecatory repression—doing it only in the right place and in the right time—is the basis of civilization. In controlling bodily desires we also learn thrift, industry, and punctuality—and, for the 'anally retentive', an obsession with money and possessions.

> *I wish I were a finger ring*
> *Upon my Lulu's hand,*
> *And every time she wiped her ass*
> *I'd see the Promised Land.*
>
> **Folk ballad.**

The human psyche is indeed complex, no more so than when we intertwine our sexual and excremental needs. Our reaction to this union is always extreme producing either repulsion or attraction. Revulsion is probably a more common reaction and many a writer and poet has pondered the cognitive dissonance between the body they love and the image of this same body doing 'it'. Three hundred years ago the poet, cleric and satirist Jonathan Swift expressed this in his poem on the marriage of Strephon when he asks a bridegroom:

> *Had you but through a cranny spied*
> *On House of Ease your future Bride,*
> *In all the posture of her face,*
> *Which Nature gives in such a case;*
> *Distortions, groanings, strainings, heavings:*
> *Your goddess grown a filthy mate.*

> *Your fancy then had always dwelt*
> *On what you saw, and what you smelt;*
> *Would still the same ideas give ye,*
> *As when you spied her on the privy.*

In another poem, Swift continue this theme, with Strephon sniffing around his love's dressing room, ending with perhaps the most famous, existential cry from the heart at his discovery of her corporeal nature.

> *So Things, which must not be exprest,*
> *When plumpt into the reeking Chest,*
> *Send up an excremental Smell*
> *To taint the parts from whence they fell.*
> *The pettycoats and gown perfume,*
> *Which waft a stink 'round every room…*
> *Thus finishing his grand survey,*
> *Disgusted Strephon stole away,*
> *Repeating in his amorous fits,*
> *Oh! Celia, Celia, Celia shits!*

Elizabeth Charlotte of the Palatine, the child bride of Louis XIV's brother, raises disgust of excrement to a new level in a letter to her aunt written in 1694:

> You see a beautiful person, neat, clean and you cry out, 'how charming it would be if she didn't shit!' I could forgive porters and soldiers and people of that ilk for doing it. But empresses shit, the Pope shits, cardinals shit, priests shit, archbishops shit, generals shit, priest and vicars shit. Admit then that the world is full of nasty people, since in truth we shit on the ground, we shit in the sea—the entire universe is full of shitters and the paths of Fontainebleau are full of big turds. If you think you are kissing a pretty little mouth with all white teeth—you are kissing a shit mill. Every single delicacy (she eats), biscuits, pastries, tarts, hams, partridges, pheasants, exists only to be made into ground up shit.

To this extraordinary letter, Aunt Sophie gives her young niece this equally extraordinary reply.

> You must have been in a bad mood when you railed against shitting...of all the necessary functions that life subjects us to, shitting is the most agreeable. There are few people who don't like the smell of their own turds...The most beautiful ladies are those who shit best; those who don't shit become dried out, skinny and as a result ugly. Shit is used to produce the best make-up. Without the dung from civet cats and other animals we would be deprived of our best perfumes. Admit that shit is the most beautiful, the most useful and pleasant thing in the world. When you don't shit you feel sluggish and in bad spirits. If you shit you feel light, happy and your appetite is good. Eating and shitting, shitting and eating, these are actions that follow each other The pleasure of shitting is so gratifying that one shits wherever one might be—in alleys, in public places on someone else's doorstep without worrying whether he likes it or not. I hope now that you regret having placed shitting in such a bad light and will agree that we would prefer death to the lack of shitting.[11]

Elizabeth Charlotte, Princess Palatine

One is curious to read more of the correspondence between these two earthy women. Put this discussion together with our image of women in the court of Louis XIV bedecked in jewels with long elegant dresses and elaborate hairdos and you see how our subject truly gives us a very different view of history.

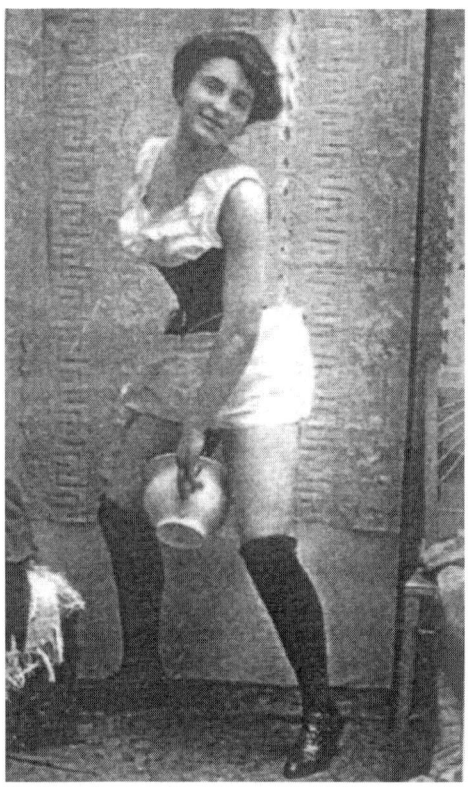

Naughty French postcard 1910

For some poets and perverts, shitting (and pissing) is precisely what excites their passion. In the fertile mind of the Marquis de Sade, watching a woman defecate was the height of sexual stimulation and in the hundreds of references to shit in *120 Days of Sodom* watching was just the appetizer.

James Joyce was similarly moved, as we see in this loving letter from him to his wife Nora:

> Remember the day you pulled your clothes off and let me lie under you looking up at you while you did it? I dream of you in filthy poses sometimes. The smallest things gives me a great cockstand. A little brown stain on the seat of your white drawers, a sudden immodest noise made by you behind and then a bad smell curling up out of your backside… It must be a fearfully lecherous thing to see a girl with her… pretty white drawers pulled open behind and her bum sticking out and a fat brown thing stuck halfway out of her hole.

Both the disgust and the titillation comes from the same place because talking or writing about the fact that we all shit is the last taboo, the most forbidden of forbidden fruits. In the end perhaps our deep skittishness about shitting is due to the fact that this act daily reminds us, as Cotton Mather observed, that we are more like animals than our pride allows us to admit. This is *the* existential predicament, a difficult fact to face, and so most of us repress it in our words, in our thoughts, and, to our ultimate disadvantage, in our actions.

Our disgust and avoidance of this subject brings with it a high cost. In her book, *The Big Necessity, The Unmentionable World of Human Waste,* Rose George passionately makes the case that millions in the world are sick or dying because we are embarrassed by the anal facts of life. The subject of building bathroom facilities and improving sanitation in the developing world is avoided by politicians, governments, and charities—yet these are the very things that could do more to promote the people's health than any other act. Celebrities will happily pose beside pumps issuing forth clean water to children in Africa but you would never see Bono or Angelina Jolie sitting in a well-constructed latrine. (Bill Gates, however, who is concerned with results not image, gives millions of dollars for projects to improve sanitation.)

While we are fixated on the dangers of terrorism, Ms. George gives the example of Pakistan, a country that spends a minuscule fraction of the money it gives to the military on sanitation—and yet this is the same country where several hundred people, at the most, die at the hands of terrorists, while 120,000 people die each year from diarrhea due to improper facilities for treating human waste. She points out that, in a world where four out of ten people still defecate in fields or by the roadside, illness due to poor sanitation kills more children than HIV, tuberculosis or malaria. These statistics do not include the hundreds of millions of people in the world who suffer from a variety of diseases, some fatal, some 'merely' debilitating, directly caused by what happens when and after they defecate. A recent study of the stools of children in Nepal found that over 70% had intestinal parasites causing anemia and general malnutrition as well as many other serious diseases.[12] Over a billion people suffer from hookworm spread by improper handling of human feces.

This is not only a Third World problem. In the United States in 2010, over 50,000 people died from colon and rectal cancer. This is one disease that is highly preventable if caught early by a regular colonoscopy examination. The preparation is unpleasant but the examination itself is painless. Our distaste and denial of all things excremental have a lot to do with many people avoiding this life-saving test. It is clear that, as individuals and as a society, our refusal to deal with shit and ass has serious and sometimes fatal consequences.

All this is perhaps justification for spending time and effort examining what, at first glance, may seem to be a silly or trivial topic. It may not have a keyword in the library, it isn't discussed in newspapers and rarely in literary works, but it is an important subject. And it is a topic that implicates both body and soul with the larger question: how clean is clean?

THE PAST STANK

Changing concepts of personal hygiene

Colonial Williamsburg advertises itself as a visit to 18th century America, and the site's curators have made every effort to recreate the experience of life in a colonial American town with minute attention to authentic details. Immaculately costumed re-creators, always in character, demonstrate different aspects of daily life as it was lived more than two centuries ago. Williamsburg leaves out one key aspect of this time-traveling experience—the smell. In past times, the cobblers and blacksmiths and particularly the candle makers and printers would have had a distinct body odor; their woolen clothing would have given off vapors; the houses and workplaces would have had their smelly spots. Their outhouses, which have been discretely omitted from the authentic historical experience, would have caused any modern visitor to gag.

It is safe to say that to the persnickety 21st century's nose, all of human history until recent times would have had a distinct and sometimes overwhelming odor. Along with the rise, fall, and rise of prudery about the human body, there was an enormous variation throughout history in standards of human cleanliness— including, inevitably, the cleanliness of the nether regions of the body. This fact remains true in many places in the world today. Notions of cleanliness are so bound up with our culture and who we are that it is difficult to see (or smell) the subject objectively. What one culture (or era of history) accepts as normal, another culture finds disgusting. When a high-born individual in colonial India first saw a British governor blow his nose and then put the dirty handkerchief back in his pocket, he had to leave the room because he felt like vomiting. Similarly, when another Indian was told that people from England wipe their behinds with a dry piece of paper after defecating, he accused his informant of spreading vicious anti-British propaganda, asserting that the Raj would never dream of performing such unsanitary practices.

When we examine the history of bathing, one of the high points of human cleanliness occurred among the wealthier classes of the Mediterranean cultures beginning before the Egyptians and continuing right through the Roman era. In these warm climates with their elaborate technology for bringing fresh water into cities and this abundance of private and public baths, these ancients were, what we might call today, cleanliness freaks. They associated bodily cleanliness with health and purity.

A Greek visitor to Egypt, the historian Herodotus—no slouch when it came to personal cleanliness himself—was amazed by the continual washing and cleaning performed daily by his Egyptian hosts. He noted with astonishment that they even washed the cups they drank out of. The priest whose job it was to be in direct contact with the gods took this concern with cleanliness to greater extremes than even the most obsessive-compulsive would do today. He would shave or pluck every hair from his body and head, cut his nails short, and bathe twice in the morning and twice at night, rinse his mouth and fumigate every orifice of his body, all this to be in a state of absolute purity while performing his religious duties. The pharaohs, being god-like themselves, were similarly scrubbed, shaved, oiled, rubbed and perfumed. And their retinue would receive the same treatment. We can assume that the odor of any upper-caste Egyptian, from King Tutankhamen to Cleopatra, would be highly pleasing to even the most discriminating modern nasal passages. We can also assume that all their orifices would similarly meet or exceed modern hygienic standards.

Upper-class Greeks and Romans and Indians would have also pleased our noses. In ancient India, men and women would brush their teeth every morning, bathe and cover their bodies with a scented paste. In the 5th century BCE, many middle class Greeks had shallow heated baths in their houses. Similar baths were to be found in their gymnasiums and temples. They built elaborate public baths with waters of various temperatures surrounded by steam rooms and large outdoor swimming pools. The Greeks were such body-beautiful enthusiasts as to put any modern Californian to shame. Their Olympics would be carried out in the nude, their spotless, muscular, well-oiled bodies on view for all (males) to see. Their statues glorify the human form and their writings expound a holistic approach to the body, the mind and the soul. Theirs was an ideology of total health, which included personal hygiene, diet, and exercise, not seen again until modern times.

The Romans, who left much of their hard thinking to the Greeks, carried on these practices. Visitors to ancient sites can still see the ruins of the public baths, public lavatories, and extensive aqueducts bringing a distant supply of fresh water into the cities. Rome even had a sewer system, the *cloasa maxima*. Ovid giving advice to his pupils said in effect, I certainly don't have to tell *you* to be clean:

> *How nearly had I warned you to beware*
> *Lest armpits smell or legs be rough with hair!*
> *As well to bid you wash your face each day,*
> *Nor leave your teeth to blacken with decay...*
> *But it's no squaws from Vaucasus that I teach...*

Water, sponges, and rag cloths as well as basins and baths were available at home for personal cleaning, and, as we shall see, the Romans were equally fastidious about anal cleaning.

But lest we get the wrong impression from the ruins of luxurious villas and the statues and the writings of the poets, we should realize that life for the average citizen, not to mention the many slaves in the ancient world, was very different. The crowded cities were hell holes of stink, filth, and disease. In the pre-industrial world, everything to make a poor person clean—soap and water and disinfectants—were rarities; even a scrap of cloth was an expensive luxury. There were open sewers and the streets were garbage dumps with little evidence of organized sanitation. Excrement and urine, rotting garbage, dead animals and even human bodies were thrown out of windows or dumped in public spaces to be scavenged by swarms of flies, packs of dogs, rats and vultures. Hollywood movies portray an ancient Rome of chariots traveling the wide streets and gatherings of proud citizens clad in flowing togas. Try for a moment to visualize the reality. Try to imagine (if you can) the smell.

The Roman historian Gaius Suetonius describes the scene of the emperor Titus Vespasian at lunch when a dog from the street comes in and deposits a human hand under the emperor's table. The historian does not register any surprise at this event but includes it in his history because it happened while an emperor was dining and so it was considered to be a bad omen.

More than a bad omen for the ordinary citizen in Rome, Athens, Cairo, Paris, London, or any crowded city until the late 1800s was the fact that they would not live very long. The Thames River, which ran through the middle of London became, in the words of the 19th century British Prime Minister, Disraeli, "a Stygian pool reeking with ineffable unbearable horror." It was the principal source of the city's drinking water but so many privies poured into it that it often ran brown, making 1858 'the year of the great stink'. The windows of the Houses of Parliament were covered with chlorine-soaked paper so the legislators could debate the idea of funding the construction of a sewer system.

Not surprisingly, childhood diseases in cities, mainly dysentery from water borne diseases, killed many infants before they were five (this remains true today in many of the poorer nations of the world). If the infants survived childhood, they would be lucky to make it past their 30's. This, in part, explains Thomas Jefferson's hatred of cities. He had seen the squalor of 18th century Paris and London and referred to New York City, the then capital of the new country, as a *cloasa* (sewer) containing all the depravities of human nature. He was instrumental in moving the capital out of town to the newly-created Washington, D.C., in a sparsely populated swamp in Virginia.

THE ODOR OF SANCTITY

Meanwhile, back in biblical times, if personal cleanliness was spotty for everyone but the middle and upper classes in Egypt, Greece, and Rome, things got considerably worse when the early Judeo-Christians got hold of the body. Josephus, the Roman historian, is both fascinated and revolted when he visits the Essenes, an ascetic sect of Judaism. "They think that oil is a defilement; and if any one of them be anointed without his own approbation, it is wiped off his body; for they think to be sweaty is a good thing."[13] The church fathers and mothers took sweatiness much further, totally condemning the practice of bathing. In part, they were reacting to the sensuality of the sweet-smelling pagans who went before them, in part they were trying to punish their bodies which they saw as the locus of all sin. As with the hippies, two millennia later, it became an act of defiance against authority *not* to wash, not to touch water according to one church authority, "even with your fingertips," preferring instead what they called the 'sweet smell of sanctity'. Long before a pilgrim came anywhere near the early Christian-saints-to-be sitting atop a pillar or living in caves, they were greeted by what one of the faithful called 'a holy odor.' In the minds of these harsh ascetics who rejected any pleasures of the body, the smellier you were, the closer you were to God. All that mattered to them was the cleanliness of your eternal soul. St. Jerome admonished his followers for frequenting the public baths, St. Catherine of Siena gave up washing, and St. Agnes never washed in her life.

An early church father, Saint Athanasius of Alexandria (293-373), instructed Christian virgins to copy the dove and take, at most, little bird baths at home with all their clothes on:

> Be like a dove. The dove is acquainted with the bath in the ordinary waters in the basin. She does not take off her garment or reveal her nudity. Observe her appearance [which] is pure, without force or cleansings.
>
> A basin is sufficient for you to wash away your dirt, Ask and learn how…Miriam sojourned in the desert without water. Have you not heard that the apostles and disciples of the Lord ate food without washing their hands? For they who were pure inside were also pure on the outside.
>
> Learn how the women who bathe have… dragged others down into corruption. The first is Bathsheba, the wife of Uriah, who, when she stripped, instantly stripped such a great man of holiness and rule… You see how she who wanted to bathe poured out filth on such a man; for because she washed her body, she defiled another's soul.[14]

Throughout the rather smelly Christian era, citizens of the Middle East kept up the ancient tradition of bodily cleanliness. In the sixth century this practice was codified with great specificity in Muslim religious teachings. Even the shape of one's fingernails was ordained:

> Believers, when you prepare for prayer, wash your faces and your hands up to the elbows, and wipe your heads and wash your feet up to the ankles... The Prophet says: "There are five things dictated by sound human nature: circumcision, removal of pubic hair, plucking of armpit hair, nail clipping, and moustache trimming". The proper healthy method of clipping one's nails is to follow the shape of the nail, which means that only the part not connected to one's skin should be clipped...
>
> When a Muslim of God's servants makes his ablution and rinses his mouth, sins come out of it, and so do they come out of his nose when he rinses it. When he washes his face, sins drop from all of his face including from behind the edges of his eyelids. When he washes his hands, sins drop from all over his hands, including from under his fingernails. When he wipes his head, they drop from his head and from under his ears. When he finally washes his feet, sins drop from them to the extent that they go out from under his toenails.[15]

As with the ancient Egyptian priests and the ancient Jews, all Muslims are required to be ritually clean before they pray to God.

> There are two types of ablution. 'abdest', the minor purification carried out before prayer, consists of washing the hands, the face, the forearms, the head and the feet. The 'Hadis' explain that by performing 'abdest' the believer washes away sin and that each drop of water that falls in the hand makes the devil flee. 'Gusül' is the major purification, which cleanses the whole body from impurities and is required after intercourse, menstruation, childbirth, before adopting Islam, and after death, but also before important celebrations and during the Hajj.[16]

The commentators point out that: "no prayers are accepted from one who has not performed ablution." And because a devout Muslim is required to pray five times a day, they were, and are, in theory at least, the cleanest people on earth. They were certainly cleaner than the average medieval Christian.

Lawrence Wright wrote that "for a thousand years Europe went unwashed," but that is not quite true. The grand medieval monasteries were located near running water and had excellent bathing facilities. The general population however, with limited access to water, did what they could to stay clean. Paris in 1292 had at least 26 guild-run bathhouses[17] and every city and town in Europe had similar bathing establishments—warm places, often located beside bakeries where people could wash and steam themselves. Either at home or communally, a Saturday bath was a tradition throughout medieval Europe. Although not bound by the stern edicts of the Muslim religion, it was a tradition for good Christians to wash off the week's sweat and grime before the holy day.

In her book *Clean,* Virginia Smith points out a surprising innovation that contributed significantly to the general personal hygiene of the era: undergarments. Medieval men and women wore close-fitting undershirts that were tied up between their legs. This undergarment, made of soft linen for the rich and rough hemp for the peasantry, enclosed and trapped all of the body's evacuations and even some of the vermin that were ever-present on the skin and in the hair. This practice may not seem very hygienic to us today but it had one important sanitary feature. Unlike their heavy woolen and leather outer garments, these undershirts could be changed and washed, and everyone but vagabonds could afford at least one change of underwear. Kings and nobles could and did change these undergarments frequently. Still, we are far from the Greek and Roman body-beautiful world of daily baths and light years from the modern world ordaining odor-free humanity.

> *By all loves soft, yet mighty powers*
> *It is a thing unfit*
> *That men should fuck in time of flowers*
> *Or when the smock's beshit*
> *Fair nasty nymph, be clean and kind,*
> *And all my joys restore;*
> *By using paper still behind,*
> *And sponges for before.*
>
> John Wilmot, the 2nd Earl of Rochester (1647-1680)

Things actually got worse after the 14th century when the plague decimated Europe. The city authorities blamed the communal public baths for causing the spread of disease and banned them. After that, most city dwellers had to be content with a splash of water.

They were not however completely oblivious to their own smell; one Elizabethan author recommended the use of perfume or the roots of certain plants to "taketh away the strong savour coming from the arm holes." Medical opinion was against the idea of a full body bathing, sternly pronouncing that total immersion was dangerous to health. Their theory was that the body's skin would absorb disease-causing agents unless protected by sweat and its natural oils. Someone's strong smell was thought to be an indication of good health. "A full-body cleansing with water became an uncommon rite, only practiced to mark a major life passage"[18] such as First Communion, marriage, and, of-course, after death. On lesser occasions, face and hands would be cleaned but the rest the body would be left untouched. The elite managed smell with powders and perfume but it was a tricky balance to maintain. Gentlemen were warned not to smell too foul like a beggar or too sweet like a harlot.

We can only imagine what it was like when all of this 'strong savour' collected together in crowds. In the pit of Shakespeare's Globe Theatre the lower class (and true 'great unwashed') were crammed together to watch the plays. They were known as the 'groundlings' or on a warm summer day the 'penny stinkards'. Vendors used to pass through balconies housing the expensive seats selling orange peels and bunches of flowers for the upper class audience members to hold to their noses to mask the terrible stink rising from the pit.

A wealthy Englishman, Sir Henry Blount (1602–1682), who traveled to the Middle East was shocked to discover that "he or she whom bathe not twice or thrice a week are held [to be] nasty." His only explanation for all this weird washing behavior was because they lived in a hot climate and—in his words—because they ate "gross food."[19]

We may ask how people could stand the terrible smells that were around them all the time—the rotting garbage, the middens (or dumps of domestic remains including excrement in the back yards), and the stink rising from their fellow humans? Sometimes they couldn't and commented on it. Consider, for example, this description by the 18th century author Tobias Smollett of the 'compound of villainous smells' at a dance in the fashionable town of Bath:

> Imagine to yourself a high exalted essence of mingled odours, arising from putrid gums, imposhhumated {abscessed} lungs, sour flatulencies, rank armpits, sweating feet, running sores, plasters, ointments, spirits of lavender, assafoetida drops {a digestive aid}, musk, hartshorn, and sal volatile, besides a thousand frousty streams which I could not analyze.[20]

Even with stink as a norm, some people, even those who could afford better, were stinkier than others. The Duke of Norfolk (1746-1815) was described by contemporaries as a vulgar, heavy, clumsy, dirty-looking mass of matter who rarely made use of water or willingly changed his linen. His servants could only sponge him down when he was totally drunk—which, fortunately, was very often. The great British lexicographer, Samuel Johnson, was equally slovenly but a stern grammarian. From this comes his (probably apocryphal) quip to a woman who told him that he smells, "I stink, madam, you smell."

Prince Leopold from the German state of Saxe-Coburg, was to be married to the future George IV's only daughter, Charlotte. If we are to believe this drawing by the satirist George Cruikshank, 'Hot Bath, or Preparations for the Wedding,' Leopold too had to be forcible held down to be bathed. The marriage, by the way, was not a happy one.

Until recently, odor was a fact of daily life and people were used to it. It just didn't have the emotional, visceral component that we experience in our hyper-clean times. Like every human sensation, smell is mediated by the brain, not by the stimulus itself but by our reaction to it. I learned this fact while researching a documentary in Kansas. My assignment was to interview a very wealthy gentleman who ran a feed lot. A feed lot is a place where cattle are collected together in huge pens and fattened before being slaughtered. When the wind is blowing in the right direction the stench, even from miles away, could make you gag. This gentleman's very luxurious house was situated miles from anywhere but right beside the feed lot. He gave me a tour of its many elegant rooms including an art studio for his wife. I was astounded both at the luxury of the house and its location. The man owned thousands of acres of land. Why did he build it there? I asked him, as diplomatically as I could, if he was bothered by the odor. He looked at me like a mentally challenged simpleton and replied, "That, young man is the smell of money!"

You may be able to get used to any odor, but the modern reader might ask how people could bear their own personal filth. With soap being a scarce commodity used for cleaning clothes, not bodies, and immersion in water being, at most, an infrequent event, discouraged by doctors and priests alike, dirtiness in the nether regions of the body was an accepted reality. From Roman times until the 19th century people would sprinkle water on their hands and face and sometimes their feet, perhaps clean their bodies with a damp cloth or sponge at the washbasin and, if they could afford it, add perfume to take care of the rest. When the middle-class Quaker woman, Elizabeth Drinker of Philadelphia, took a shower in 1799 it was an event worthy of an entry in her diary: "I went into the shower bath. I bore it better than I expected, not having been wett all over att once, for 28 years past."

Country folk were even more reluctant to immerse their bodies in water. In 1852 Henry Thoreau wrote in his diary:

> I am inclined to think bathing almost one of the necessaries of life but its surprising how indifferent some are to it. Farmers who are in most need of it rarely dip their bodies into the streams or ponds. [One] was telling me last night that he had thought of bathing when he had done [the season's] hoeing—of taking some soap and going down to the pond and giving himself a good scrubbing—but something had occurred to prevent it, and now he will go unwashed to the harvesting, aye, even till the next hoeing is over.

The more we learn about history the more we realize that the past was a very different world. One thing is for certain; with the dirt, the smells, the lice, the intestinal worms and personal vermin of all sorts, not to mention the disease, we wouldn't be very happy back then.

The modern sweeter smelling world of personal cleanliness began in earnest as an upper-class-woman thing in France in the mid 18th century. To take baths, to clean one's entire body including one's lower regions, became one of the ways that the French nobility differentiated themselves from the great unwashed peasantry. Among female aristocrats, daily bathing became a regular activity, the *Cabinet de Bain* became an essential room in which every chateau and hôtel de ville were fitted with luxurious baths and bath accessories. This habit of regular bathing spread to some men, and to aristocratic wannabes like the French revolutionaries (Marat was assassinated while luxuriating in his bath). England, always resistant to anything continental, came to body cleanliness by another route. As colonial rulers in India, the Raj quickly learned that perfect body cleanliness was a requirement of every upper-caste Indian. They went native, adopting customs like taking showers and an Indian invention, the daily '*champu*,' and ended up bringing these habits back to their much dirtier countrymen at home.

In the late 19th century, when clean running water, and extensive plumbing came into many homes, and industrially manufactured soap became inexpensive, regular full body washing was taken up by the middle class.

The final push into the bathtub, at least in Europe and America, came about because of the dual forces of science and rapacious capitalism. It began in the 1870s with the most successful and long-running campaign in the history of advertising; the selling of Pears' Soap. This gentle transparent soap had been manufactured in limited quantities since the 18th century, but in the mid 19th century the company pioneered a way of selling it to the masses. On billboards, painted on the sides of buildings, in newspapers and magazines, few Britishers could escape the phrase or the implication of the slogan repeated endlessly. *'Good Morning. Have you used Pears' soap?'* The company even tried, unsuccessfully, to get their slogan printed on the back of postage stamps.

Ten years later, Ivory Soap mounted a similar campaign in the United States. Sold initially as laundry soap, it soon found an even larger market.

A reader today may not appreciate the full meaning of the following ad but this is the 19th century vision of liberated women. Everything in this image would be new and almost shocking to Victorian readers: the women wearing bloomers instead of tight corsets, allowing their bodies to move freely, the very idea of women exercising and even sweating, the talk of hard muscles in the copy, and finally the idea of washing one's body with soap—all these were revolutionary ideas.

> WHAT sensations are more agreeable than those following some good, quick exercise, a rub with a rough towel, a scrub with Ivory Soap and a dash of cold water? The nerves are braced, the muscles are hardened, and the man or woman is better able to resist disease

Along with industrially mass produced soap, science and technology in the late 19th century transformed people's lives with a tsunami of inventions and discoveries that we continue to experience today. If we imagine *our* lives to have been completely altered by computers and cell phones, think of this: until the end of the Victorian era, people really didn't know what caused disease and could do little to avoid sickness. Epidemics regularly swept through cities, killing off at least a tenth of the population. If you cut your finger you could very well die from the infection. Any one of a myriad of illness whose terror is almost forgotten today—diphtheria, plague, cholera, even measles—might end your life.

Tuberculosis, for example, killed one in four adults in Europe in the 19th century; one in five children died in their first year of infant diarrhea.

People had many theories about the causes of illness—bad air or bad blood or simply the will of God—but were virtually powerless to do much about it. Some theorists had hit on the idea that micro-organisms cause disease but the 'animacular hypothesis' was one theory among many and not widely accepted. It seemed illogical that something that you couldn't even see could make you sick. In the 1840s, the Hungarian physician, Ignaz Semmelweis, observed that his fellow doctors were causing massive deaths on his Vienna obstetrical ward. It was common practice for them to go directly from the dissecting room to examine the open wounds of their women patients without properly washing their hands. For his theory that dirty hands were causing sickness, Semmelweis was so ridiculed by the medical establishment that he ended up his days raving mad in a mental institution.

Then, in the late 1800s, came the undeniable proof that germs caused disease. The German researcher, Robert Koch, developed a way of actually seeing and being able to identify the microscopic organisms that would periodically wipe out much of the human race. In ten short years, Louis Pasteur and other researchers located the invisible killers for diseases from typhoid to gonorrhea. Before the discovery of bacteria, surgery often was a death sentence. Now with sterilization of hands and instruments, complex surgical interventions became life-saving. Understanding these micro-organisms led to vaccines and an insistence on the purification of water, two interventions that have done more to extend human life than anything medical science has done since.

This began what one writer called 'the gospel of germs' and it also led to a drastic, often irrational change in personal habits. Washing and smelling sweet now became a medical necessity—a matter of life and death. A writer in a popular magazine insisted that the "war of the body against invading germs is a great battle that one is called upon to fight continually throughout life." This belief changed the design of homes and the cleaning of homes. Dust was presented as not merely dirty but as deadly. Laundry must not only be washed: it had to be sterilized. And, as we shall see, this war on microbes revolutionized everything connected with that dirtiest of the dirtiest, the business of defecation.

Fixed bathtubs began to enter American households in the 19th century—but very slowly. In 1860, for example, there were only 4000 tubs to immerse Boston's 178,000 citizens. The number of tubs began to increase dramatically towards the end of the century but these were generally located in the kitchen near a source of water heating on the stove. It is surprising to realize that the modern bathroom with a tub, a sink, and a toilet is a recent innovation. It wasn't until the mid 20th century that a majority of homes in the United States had such a room.

Along with the discovery of germs came an understanding of contagion and an appreciation that disease knows no boundaries. The iceman or grocer handling your food could and did bring these invisible killers into even the most elegant homes. Suddenly responsibility for waging the war on germs expanded to include not only individual households but also public health departments. Now even the poor were subjected to regular scrubbings paid for by germ-conscious middle-class voters. And because they did not have indoor plumbing, as in ancient Greece and Rome, public baths began to be built in cities in England and America.

> By 1897... personal cleanliness had become a necessity... If slum tenements failed to provide the poor with bathing facilities so that they could attain the proper standards of cleanliness, then cities must provide public baths to wash the great unwashed. Cleanliness had become a right of all citizens.[21]

We have come a long way in 100 years and perhaps have overshot the mark. The natural oils and the protective bacteria that give us a healthy skin are harmed by too much soap and the widespread use of disinfectants promotes the evolution of even uglier bugs, but this medical fact has not reached the general public. Most people are still infected with the early 20th century idea that all germs everywhere must be destroyed at all cost. Did manufacturers and advertisers jump on this anti-germ hysteria to sell their products? You bet.

They hounded housewives with the message that 'mere' cleanliness was not enough. Household disinfectants became big business, as did water filters, room fumigators, insecticides, and paper towels. Cellophane was invented to cover food, along with sanitary drinking fountains, pasteurized milk, and canned meats. America had declared total war on germs and the front line was the human body.

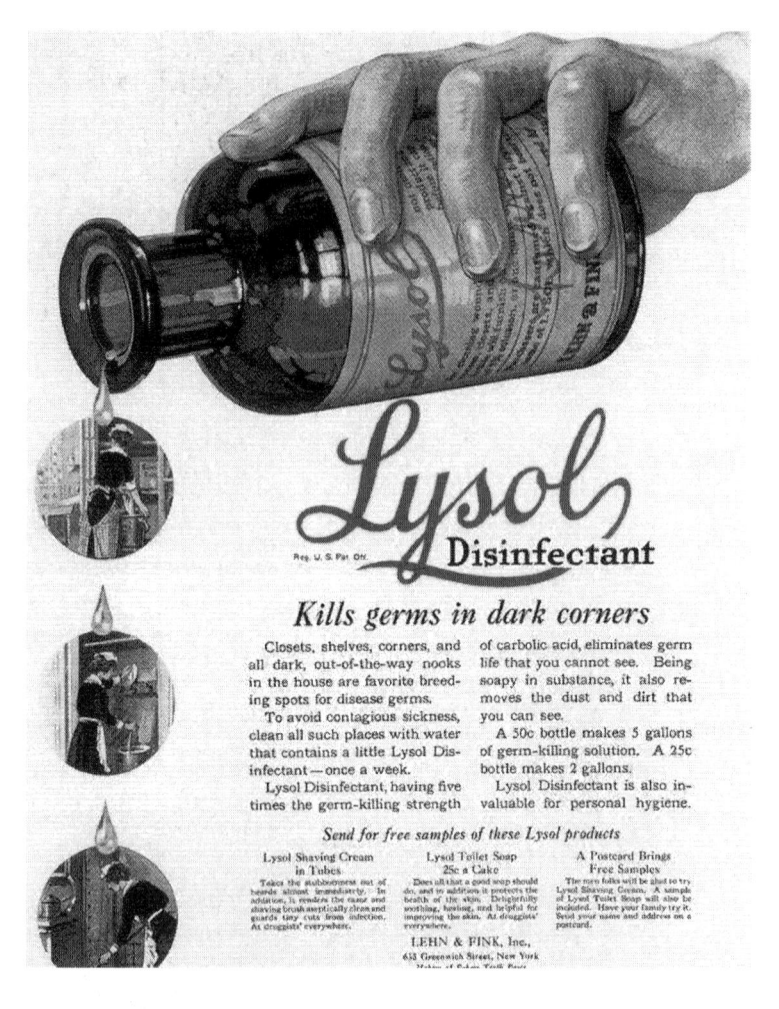

It was now no longer enough for a person to be dipped into a tub only once a week, and no orifice could escape the potions of the retailers. Mouth-washes were invented to neutralize any evil animalcules hiding in your mouth, creams to kill their cousins lurking between your toes—neither ears, nor noses, nor throats, nor crotches were to be left in peace.

Then came the march of the deodorants...

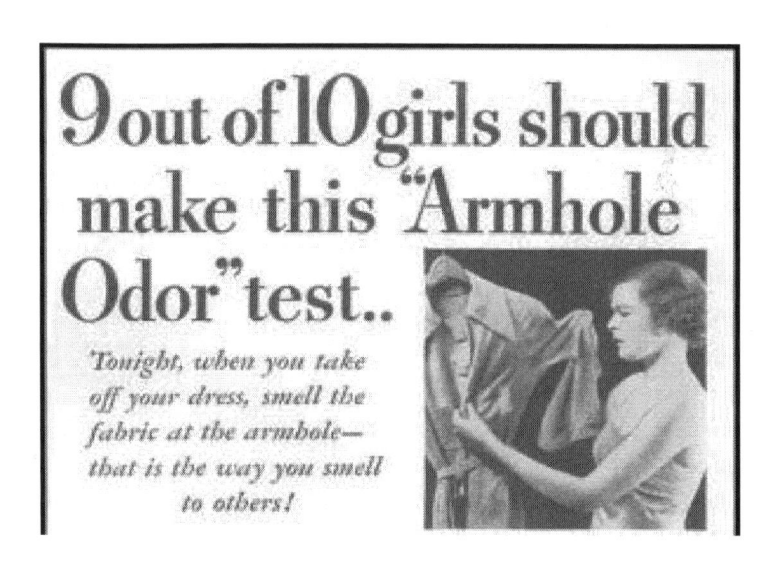

9 out of 10 girls should make this "Armhole Odor" test..

Tonight, when you take off your dress, smell the fabric at the armhole— that is the way you smell to others!

> As the party goes on, people leave Ann alone. And she doesn't know why.

For a century the drumbeat continued in every magazine, on billboards, radio and then on television: everyone had to be clean and odor-neutral. Europeans were slow to get the message, and many bodies in other parts of the world have yet to be disinfected. But amazingly, until very recently, this message also failed to penetrate every pore and orifice of the American body politic. I am old enough to remember a time when some perfectly respectable people had an air about them. And it wasn't at all unpleasant; it was who they were.

A REFRESHER ON TOILETS

Charles V, the future Holy Roman Emperor, was born on one in 1500; 477 years later, Elvis Presley died on one. Throughout human history, the toilet and its predecessors are filled with such stories of both life and death.

We have many excellent histories about the place or thing into which we defecate, which we now call by the euphemism 'toilet'. One is the delightful but mainly fictional *Flushed with Pride, The story of Thomas Crapper, inventor of the flushing toilet.* Although our interest is laser-focused on the specific post-pooping activity of humankind, we briefly deal with the history of toilets here because it is essential to get an overview of the various environments through history in and on which butts were cleaned.

Defecation receptacles have taken every form imaginable but they all have one common feature. They are all designed to transport our shit from where we are to where we aren't—to remove our excreta from where we live. However we did it, be it with a hole in the ground, a drop on the side of a castle, a container that is taken away or a sewer system flushed by water, throughout history, we find the universal desire to get the stuff out of sight and smell as quickly as possible. The most dramatic and nauseating demonstration of this fact is the use of the so-called helicopter toilet in the over-crowded and under-bathroomed cities of Africa. There millions of people regularly defecate into a plastic bag, tie it up, and throw it out the window, by the road or onto the neighbor's roof. It may not make for a very pleasant urban landscape but this method certainly serves the function of transporting feces from its source to somewhere else.

One thing becomes apparent as this story unfolds: every culture and every different period of history has strongly held views on where and how shitting takes place. What one culture might see as progress, another abhors. Our own way is imprinted on us from childhood, and we viscerally consider any variations on the theme practiced by others to be completely revolting. If all your life you are used to squatting over a hole in the ground and cleaning yourself with your hand, you will react with disgust when presented with a shiny white porcelain receptacle and its accompanying roll of paper. Change of any kind comes slowly because, as we shall see, in matters of the ass we are all deeply conservative

OPEN DEFECATION

In the beginning there were, of course, neither toilets nor bathrooms; there was just the ground below. For many people today, that remains a defecatory fact of life. Some people living in rural areas still prefer to 'go' in the fields. It has the multiple advantages of being convenient and (in their view) more hygienic than any dirty, smelly, confined alternatives near home. It also makes the corn grow. What is most surprising is that open defecation is still the norm today, not only in the countryside but in the teeming cities of Africa and India. Shit and shitting are everywhere, by the roadside, in the road, by railroad tracks, and in alleyways. In her book, *The Big Necessity*, Rose George gives us the astounding statistics about India: "Every day, 200,000 tons of human feces are deposited in India. I don't mean that they are dealt with or sent down sewers…These 155,000 truckloads are left in the open to be trodden on, stepped over, and lived among." [22]

The explanation for this fact is, in part, poverty and lack of alternatives but also, in part, the population's innate anal conservativeness. To combat this problem, the government had constructed millions of public latrines out of brick and cement but the population saw these structures as nicer than their own homes. They were promptly occupied as storerooms for firewood, goat sheds, and bedrooms. Many Indians wouldn't dream of using such fine buildings as toilets when the side of the road would suffice. Even when used for their designated purpose, these government latrines were soon abandoned and for good reason; try to imagine what it would be like in India's torrid climate to have to spend any time in a dark, fetid, 120 degree concrete box. Squatting down in the shade of a nice cool tree is infinitely more desirable. There is even the story of a wealthy farmer living in a luxurious home who, every morning, would pack his family into his fancy car and drive into the countryside so everyone could do it *au naturel*.

Throughout history to today, city planners, sanitarians, and toilet paper manufactures are constantly butting up against the fact that we are all extremely reluctant to change our bathroom habits.

The concept of the indoor toilet is nothing new. They are found in the ruins of Babylonian palaces built 2300 BCE. The palace of the legendary King Minos on the island of Crete, built around 1500 BCE, has over 1400 hundred rooms adorned with columns, paintings including 'toilet' rooms complete with wooden seats. The royal waste would be washed down and away through an elaborate system of terracotta pipes.

Chinese tombs, like those of the ancient Egyptians, included all the comforts of home for use in the afterlife. In a 2000-year-old tomb in the Chinese central province of Henan, archaeologists have unearthed a toilet truly fit for an emperor fitted with armrests and provisions for running water underneath.

The ancient Jews, a nomadic people with little access to running water, had no such luxury but were commanded by the word of God Himself to take care of their poop—or else. Consider Deuteronomy chapter 23:

> Designate a place outside the camp where you can go to relieve yourself. As part of your equipment have a spade to dig with, and when you relieve yourself, dig a hole and cover up your excrement. For the LORD your God moves about in your camp to protect you and to deliver your enemies to you. Your camp must be holy, so that he will not see among you anything indecent and turn away from you.

Why does Vacerra spend his hours
In all the privies, and day-long sit?
He wants a supper, not a shit.
               Marcus Valerius Martialis (40 – 103 AD)

Public Latrine in Ostia, near Rome.

The Greeks and later the Romans had both private latrines at home connected to a sewer system and most notably elaborate public lavatories or *foricea*. As noted in the open of this book, these were convivial gathering places to gossip or conduct business. Some had as many as 60 seats arranged in a rectangle or semicircle, and people would defecate in full view of one another. The idea of having privacy while we shit or pee, although it may seem an absolute necessity to modern Western men and women, is a relatively new concept. For most of our history we all did it unabashedly in public.

Even in private houses, men and women regarded defecating as a time to commune with friends or family. Archeologists have unearthed three, five, even seven seaters in Roman villas. The practice of pooping together continued until early modern times. In his advice on manners, the British author Thomas Dekker (1570-1641) told his readers that "you may invite some special friend of yours from the table to hold discourse with you as you sit in that with-drawing chamber." And people did so withdraw. After dinner, well into the 19th century, it was men to their cigars and chamber pots, women to theirs.

This lack of privacy is immortalized in a 2000-year-old fresco recently uncovered at Ostia Antica, the ancient seaport of Rome. In a room in the 'Bath of the Seven Sages,' we see, along the lower wall, portraits of men doing their business in the multi-seated latrine and above, sitting in their Grecian chairs, seven august philosophers giving scatological wisdom to the patrons below. The philosopher Solon advises them *"ut bene cacaret ventrem palpavit"* (to shit well you should rub your belly). The Milesian sage, Thales urges them to push hard and the bearded philosopher Chion of Sparta instructs them on how to fart without making a sound—*Vissire tacite Chilon docuit subdolus.* Another philosopher whose name has, alas, not been preserved gives the adage *"amice fugit te proverbium /bene caca et irrima medicos."* (Hey friend, shit well and make the doctors give you a blow job—meaning screw doctors because if you shit well, you won't need them.) All this wise advice is putting pressure on the defecators below. One man is saying to another, "I'm hurrying up!" Thales also tells the sitters that no one will criticize them if they wipe themselves well.[23]

Both the ancient world and the medieval world made use of chamber pots, earthenware containers with a wide base and a narrower opening at the top over which the user would squat and do his or her business. Sometimes with equipped with a cover, chamber pots were often stored under the bed or in a piece of furniture. Their content would be dumped, along with other refuse in midden piles in the backyard, in a river (if one was nearby), or, as depicted in many illustrations, it would be poured out the nearest window. If the pourer were polite, he or she would first call out '*gardez l'eau*!' (French for 'watch out for the water!') from which it is believed that the British derived both the word 'loo' for bathroom and the custom of wearing wide-brimmed hats.

Sometime in the late Middle Ages, the elite decided that having these stinky things underfoot did not fit in with the latest in medieval interior decor. Also, squatting and aiming at a chamber pot could be a hit-and-miss affair, so furniture makers came up with a device called a 'close-stool'.

The close-stool is a wooden box with a hole in the top. The chamber pot would reside inside the box. The user would sit comfortably on top, sometimes on a padded seat, and the contents of his or her bowels would miraculously disappear below. A side door would allow servants to take out the chamber pot and empty its contents. It may have started out as a simple wooden box, but, as its users rose in status so did its design.

This is Henry VIII's close-stool with silver handles and a red velvet cushioned seat. It also featured a hinged top with a lock on it so no one but the royal ass would have access to it.

And here Louis XV shat, in the splendor of Versailles.

Elizabeth I, who frequently traveled the country, ordered a portable close-stool to be built, covered with black embroidered velvet decorated with ribbon and gilt nails. The seat was scarlet velvet fringed with silk and gold threads. The pan was pewter.

Her transport included a 'close-carriage' where the item was always ready nearby because, as one writer commented, the Queen could hardly nip behind a bush.[24]

As befits a humble servant of the church, the Vatican Museum has this simple wooden example of the Pope's close-stool—known by its Latin name *sedia stercoraria,* the pierced chair. It is an object that also serves an important role in the Catholic ritual. In 855 AD Pope John VIII was elected Pontiff. Later it was discovered that Pope John was really Pope Joan much to the embarrassment of the Church which claims to have an unbroken "boy's club" of Popes right back to the apostle St. Peter. To detect any possible future female imposters, all subsequent potential Popes were required to sit on the sedia stercoraria before ordination to be officially felt up by a church official.

The caption coming out of the mouth of the Papal Groper in this illustration by a Swedish witness to the 1644 ordination of Pope Innocent X reads in Latin: "The Pontiff has them," much to the relief of the assembled multitude.

In private homes, human ingenuity in concealing these offensive objects showed great creativity. Here is a British close-stool camouflaged as a pile of books, entitled, appropriately for English rears, *The Mysteries of Paris,* in four fat volumes.

When it came to ornate close-stools, the upper class could not resist outdoing one another. Madame de Pompadour, (1721-1764) Louis XV's mistress, had her close-stool decorated with gold embroidered blue velvet. The device even had arms and feet inlaid with gold and the seat was covered with Moroccan leather. Even the unseen chamber pots could not be left unadorned. From rough earthenware they evolved into gleaming white porcelain objets d'art painted with the family's coat of arms on the side. For the upper, upper class they were made of pure silver and, yes, even gold for royalty.

In a trend we shall also see with toilet paper, chamber pots took on humorous and political themes. The Duke of Wellington had a pot inscribed with a cartoon of a grinning man captioned:

Keep me clean and use me well,
And what I see, I will not tell.

When Benjamin Franklin came to France in the 1780s he was lionized by the intelligentsia. Like a modern-day rock star, entrepreneurs sold his portrait everywhere and on everything. Louis XVI, who thought that his image should be everywhere, was getting a little jealous and so he had Franklin's portrait emblazoned on the bottom of his mistress's chamber pot.

Louis used to conduct some of the kingdom's business sitting on this particular throne and it was considered a great privilege by members of the inner circle, to be admitted in the morning to the King's private chambers while he was very publicly doing the King's business. In the American White House of the 1960s, President Lyndon Johnson carried on this tradition. This was in line with his theory of leadership. He once told a potential applicant for a job as his assistant: "I don't want loyalty, I want LOYALTY. I want you to kiss my ass in Macy's window at high noon and tell me it smells like roses." The toilet had indeed become a very public seat of power.

In the 16th century, defectory behavior was beginning to change. We see this change depicted in a series of book on manners which were becoming popular at the time. The following is from a book published in 1558:

> It is not proper to hold out the stinking thing for the other to smell, as some are wont to do, or to lift the foul-smelling thing to his nostrils saying 'I should like you to know how much that stinks. It would be much better to say, 'because it stinks do not smell it.' [25]

It is likely that the author feels he must tell his readers what not to do, precisely because many people *were* doing it. This from manner books published in 1570 and in 1589:

> One should not, like rustics who have not lived among refined people, relieve oneself without reserve in front of ladies or before the doors or windows of [someone's] room.

Let no one, whoever he may be, before, at, or after meals, foul the staircases, corridors or closets with urine or other filth, but go to suitable prescribed places for such relief.[26]

Even before modern times however, there were indications that everyone was not totally comfortable crapping in the public eye or anywhere else they pleased. They did have alternatives. Unlike today, large cities had public toilets, or rather traveling human public toilets. In Paris and other European cities, enterprising men would carry buckets and large cloaks and travel the streets calling out their services, *"Chacun sait se qu'il à faire et il faut payer deux sous* [27]*,"* (Everyone knows what he needs to do and you have to pay two cents.). For the price of admission, you would sit on his bucket and he would surround you with the cloak for a moment of privacy and relief.

Beginning around the 1600s the prescribed places for such relief in some British homes became a closet—a small room where they would install their close-stools or chamber pots. They were proud, in a British way, of their sophistication, as represented in a 1796 cartoon by the satirist James Gillray.

In his illustration, titled, *'National Conveniences,'* the Scotch do it in a bucket, the French in a filthy latrine, the Dutch sitting on a fence feeding ducks in a lake, while a beef-fed John Bull grunts his all in the luxury of a private closet.

This peculiar British taste for defecatory privacy may go back to a time of knights in armor living in castles. In the middle ages your regulation castle often boasted a separate room jutting out of the walls like a turret. Often built near fireplaces or above kitchens, they caught the heat from the rising fires to warm those cold stone seats. From this room euphemistically called a *garderobe* (French for a clothes closet), waste dropped several hundred feet into the moat below. No problem with back splash, but visitors at the castle gates would be greeted with a terrible smell and see the telltale brown stains dribbling down the walls of these imposing structures. The savory contents of the moat, however, may have stopped any potentially invading army in its tracks.

In the way that even today we assign things that we find distasteful to another country, when the French built separate rooms for defecation they called them *lieux à l'anglaise* (English places).

The Middle Ages were a turbulent time for kings who always had to be on guard for internal as well as external enemies. The dung-encrusted chute leading out of the *garderobes* were frequently used as a way of making a quick exit during these perennial insurrections.

We are all vulnerable with our underwear down below our knees sitting on a toilet. There are many Internet tales (some may even be true) of rats or squirrels coming up through the toilet and biting an exposed behind, but none of this imagined horror can match a true-life toilet story told in the *Chronicle History of England* by Henry of Huntington (d. 1154). In 1016, England was divided between two rivals, King Edmund and Cnut the Great, who was also King of Denmark. The two maintained an uneasy peace and Edmund, a fierce warrior himself, and well-guarded by an entourage of bodyguards, felt pretty safe at home in his castle. But, as Henry of H tells the story:

> Thus it happened: one night, this great and powerful king having occasion to retire to the house for relieving the calls of nature, Edric, concealed himself in the pit, and stabbed the king twice from beneath with a sharp dagger, and, leaving the weapon fixed in his bowels, made his escape. Edric then presented himself to Cnut, and saluted him, saying, 'Hail! Thou who art sole king of England!' Having explained what had taken place, Cnut replied, "For this deed I will exalt you as it merits, higher than all the nobles of England." He then commanded that Edric should be decapitated and his head placed upon a pole on the highest battlement of the tower of London.

Even back then the end did not justify the means. Cnut considered that hiding in someone's toilet and stabbing him upward through the gut at the moment when he was least able to defend himself was not cricket.

You can be sure that future Kings of England looked before they sat.

Brisk-CATHARTIC.

In these garderobes and privies of the nobility, we have the ancestors of the modern bathroom, but there were many slips twixt the cup and that porcelain lip.

The first actual flush toilet, with a bowl and source of water to clean it out, was devised around 1596 by Sir John Harington (1561 - 1612) for use by his godmother, Queen Elizabeth I. In a book called *A New Discourse upon a Stale Subject*, he diagrammed his creation, calling it "a privie in perfection" with its flushed-out bowl "to keep all sweet and savourie."

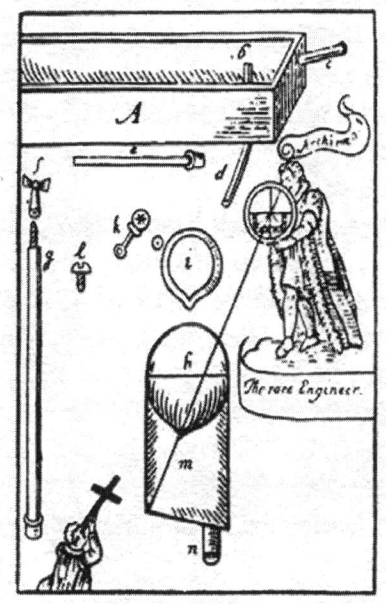

This is Don Ajax house...all in sunder; that a workman may see what he hath to do

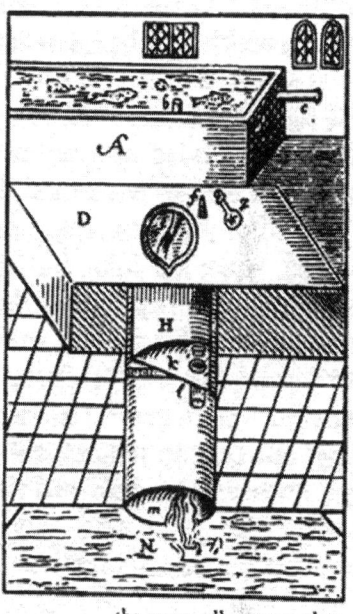

...the same, all put together, that the workman may see if it be well

Harington's Watercloset, 1596. From his *Metamorphosis of Ajax*

- A,   The Cistern: stone or brick.
- b, d, e   the pipe that comes from the cistern with a stopple to the washer
- c,   a waste pipe
- f, g   the item of the great stopple with a key to it
- h,   the form of the upper brim of the vessel or stool pot
- m,   the stool pot of stone
- n,   the great brass sluice, to which if three inches current to send it down a gallop into the JAX
- i,   the seat, with a peak devant for elbow room

Sir John was about 250 years ahead his time. His invention would have to wait for an era of sewers and piped-in supplies of running water. Also, one major aspect of toilet technology had yet to be solved. If you were going to have this contraption in your house and the waste was going to flow into a cesspool or a sewer, you absolutely needed some way of stopping the gases from the decomposition of fecal matter from backing up into the house. In an era when bad air was thought to be the cause of all disease this was all the more important, not to mention the fact that the main component of sewer gas is methane, which could explode and blow up the house. People attempted to install a moving metal valve which would seal up the drain, but these contrivances inevitably became clogged up or began to leak.

The hero of modern toilet technology is this dour-looking Scottish watchmaker, Alexander Cummings (1733-1814) who in 1775 took out patent number 814, an event that would change the world.

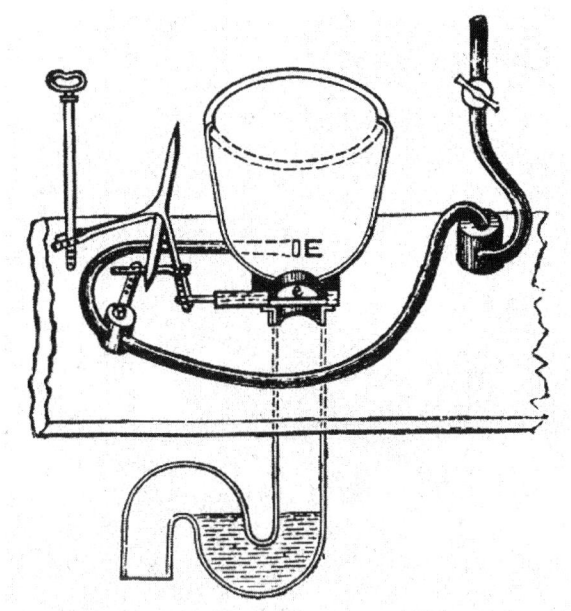

Cumming's simple but brilliant idea was connecting the so-called 'S valve' to the bottom of the bowl. By configuring the pipes in this way the water itself would seal the toilet off from the gases below.

Cummings' Valve closet, 1775

Since 1775 almost every aspect of our technological world has completely changed except this one. If you were to take apart the flush toilet in your bathroom or any one of the billions such toilets in the world you still would find, unaltered for 235 years, the same 'S valve' conceived by that dour Scottish watchmaker.

With all these wonderful creations, the porcelain chamber pots, the ornate close-stools, and the beginnings of the modern flush toilet, called the *water* closet; it may surprise the modern reader to learn that, in the most elegant palaces and ballrooms, from the Renaissance well into the 19th century, people were still doing it on the floor.

The diarist Anthony Wood (1632-1695) describes the Court of Charles II.

> To give a further character of the court, though they were neat and gay in apparel yet they were very nasty and beastly, leaving at their departure their excrements in every corner, in chimneys, studies, coalhouses, and cellars.

In the splendor of Versailles, with its shining chandeliers and its Hall of Mirrors, we have many accounts of what was happening on the ground. Here is one from the sister-in-law of Louis XIV dated July 23, 1702:

> There is one dirty thing at Court that I shall never get used to: the people stationed in the galleries in front of our rooms piss and shit into all the corners. It is impossible to leave one's apartments without seeing somebody pissing.

The writer Turmeau de La Morandière describes the Versailles of Louis XV as "the receptacle of all of humanity's horrors, the passageways, corridors and courtyards are full of urine and fecal matter." The elegant formal gardens outside the royal palace were deliberately planted with tall hedges to be used as de facto bathroom stalls. And in Frederick the Great of Prussia's magnificent palace, *Sans Souci,* there was a notice in the grand entrance begging courtiers to please not urinate or defecate on the stairs.

In the 19th century, Lord Byron was banned from Long's Hotel on London's Bond Street for constantly using a corner of the foyer rather than bothering to go down to the basement latrines. And then there was the following notice posted in a London gentleman's club:

During the asparagus season, members are kindly requested not to relieve themselves in the hat stand.

Gentlemen, the nobility, and royalty had a bevy of servants to clean up their mess. For humbler folk, the fireplace was the place of choice into which to relieve themselves when they were too lazy to reach for the chamber pot.

> *If spitting chance to move thee so*
> *Thou canst it not forbeare,*
> *Remember do it modestly,*
> *Consider who is there.*
>
> *If filthiness or ordure thou*
> *Upon the floore doe cast,*
> *Thread out and cleanst it with thy foot,*
> *Let that be done in haste*
>
> Richard West, The Book of Demeanour (1619)

Flush toilet technology advanced rapidly in the 19th century but people strongly resisted having the receptacle of defecation take up permanent residence in the private home. As one 19th century architect grumbled:

> A fashion prevails of thrusting these noisome things into the midst of sleeping chambers and living rooms—pandering to effeminacy and, at times, surcharging the house—for they cannot, at all times, and under all circumstances, be kept perfectly close—with their offensive odor. Out of the house they belong, and if they, by any means, find their way within its walls proper, the fault will not be laid at our door.[28]

Outhouses could be okay when the weather was fine but as one commentator, James C. Baynes, noted: "a visit to an outdoor privy in a cold storm or when the ground is covered with snow and the air frosty is attended with a physical shock which even strong men dread." He cited this dread of outhouses as a major cause of constipation in women. But indoor flush toilets need a lot of water, and so they had to wait for the establishment of a reliable supply of piped water. The business end could be fed into cesspools but the system really became practical and maintenance free only when the flush toilet could be connected to a sewer system.

According to U.S. Census figures, until 1940, most Americans continued to 'go to the bathroom' in an outhouse.

Working class housing, Cincinnati 1935.
Note the outhouses in the back alley.

In an outhouse, you would sit on a wooden seat and your waste would fall (sometimes not very far) into a cesspit below. The tiny building would adjoin the house or stand in the back alley. Far from the romanticized outhouse in the woods, in the crowded slums of London, Paris, and New York communal privies would serve many families and, like many things communal these necessaries were rarely cleaned. One social reformer who ventured into one of these places in the slums of London described it as "one of the most horrible examples of loathsomeness and indecency that I have ever experienced."

Landlords were supposed to have the pits cleaned out regularly but, like landlords everywhere, they would save money by waiting until the pit was "full and overflowing, covering the yard with its putrescent filth."[29]

American reformers took these photographs of typical privies behind New York slums to inspire the city fathers to pass bylaws outlawing them.

Apart from the horrifying aesthetic and olfactory experience that these urban privies offered their clients, they were also a major health hazard. The receiving pits below the outhouses were often deliberately left only partly lined with mortar so that the liquid portion of the sewage would seep into the ground, thus saving money by requiring a less frequent cleaning out of the pit. The overflow of the cesspits however, contaminated the drinking water with fecal organisms. The result: horrible epidemics of cholera and dysentery which sickened or killed millions.

When the microbial mechanism of disease was finally understood towards the end of the 19th century, sewers and a clean water supply became an imperative in large cities. The flush toilet, with its so-called wash-out bowl, was ready for its close-up.

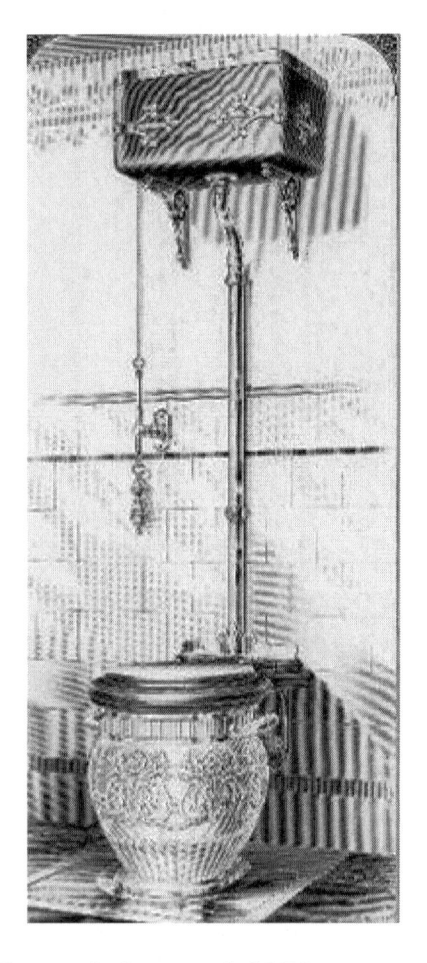

The period around 1870 represents a frenzy of activity in the field of toilet technology. The objective was to construct a simple, maintenance free device, with a bowl that, in effect, would clean itself after every flush. It also must not clog or admit smell from the sewers. In the Health Exhibition held in London in 1884, the Pedestal Vase perfected by the greatest Victorian sanitary engineer, Josiah George Jennings, out-flushed them all and won the gold medal by downing, in one gulp, ten apples, one sponge, four pieces of paper, and an oily substance that had been smeared on the bowl.

Now, at last, the object with the unmentionable name could be admitted into the most elegant family home. And so the pedestal toilet was born.

'Pedestal Lion' Closet

'The Lambeth', 1895

'Mulberry Peach Decoration', 1890

Despite all this porcelain elegance, however, there was one more problem to solve. The appropriately named 'Deluge' and other similar models required a deluge of water to perform their miraculous act of cleaning and carrying away the bowlful of waste. When you pulled the chain above these wondrous devices, the entire house shook with the thunderous force of the water surging from the tank above. Imagine a Victorian woman's horror knowing that the entire household and probably some of the neighbors were hearing that she had just taken a dump. Enter American ingenuity. "You surely know the embarrassment of a noisy bath room closet," especially in front of guests, intones the ads by Trenton Potteries.

> YOU surely know the embarrassment and annoyance a noisy bath room closet causes. Do you know that such a nuisance positively *can be avoided*? There is a closet which, when properly installed with the fittings intended for it, operates so quietly that it can scarcely be heard a few feet away, and not at all outside the bath room. It is the
>
> TRENTON POTTERIES COMPANY
>
> **SIWELCLO** NOISELESS SIPHON JET **CLOSET**
>
> the one closet which was designed primarily to be noiseless, but its sanitary features have in no way been overlooked; it flushes thoroughly, has the approved deep water seal, etc.
>
> The Siwelclo is made of Trenton Potteries Vitreous China, a material so impervious that even when the glaze is removed, no acid or color will penetrate it.
>
> Your architect and plumber will tell you there is nothing better than Trenton Potteries Company Vitreous China for sanitary fixtures.
>
> *Send for our Booklet S 5 "Model Bath Rooms of Character"*
> You will find in it many suggestions for the outfitting of bath rooms both large and small.
>
> **THE TRENTON POTTERIES COMPANY,** Trenton, N. J., U. S. A.
> The Largest Manufacturers of Sanitary Pottery in the U. S. A.

By 1913 they had it all figured out. By leaving water standing in the bowl, and changing the configuration of the 'S' trap, the flush could be much less forceful while at the same time effectively removing all waste and leaving a clean bowl. Siwelclo also eliminated the tank above which had supplied the older models with their deluge of water. The result was a neat, compact self-contained unit. The toilet became a standard in millions of American households; in older homes, there still exist today some of the original models built in the teens of the 20th century still happily flushing into the teens of 21st century.

Today, we can all sit proudly on our magnificent thrones of Victorian technology. Completely free of dirt and smell we are prepared to enter society almost free of shame. But, as stated in the timeless advice from the philosopher Thales on that 2000 year-old fresco on the Roman wall: shame free, only after we have wiped ourselves well.

4 BEFORE PAPER

We are the only animal with fat, deep buttocks that gives us a wonderful gift, a cushion when we sit. Because of this useful piece of anatomy—the gluteus maximus—we are also the only animal that dirties the interior cheeks of these well-padded buttocks when we defecate. But unlike any respectable dog or rabbit, even the supplest yogi does not have the ability to lick his own anus. So we humans have always had a problem: how to clean out the residue of our defecation. Along with language, music, and the ability to think in the future tense, anal cleaning is one of the universals of being human. From the beginning of time, we have used our collective human ingenuity towards this end and we have come up with a surprising variety of means.

How exactly we did it, however, is not easy to discover, due to the paucity of primary sources and archaeological artifacts, so this tale can only be seen in fragments. A document here or a sentence there will—like the flash from a camera—briefly illuminate this secret world and then, often for centuries, the subject will fall into darkness

We do not know how early Homo sapiens sapiens wiped her or his prehistoric ass. Surprisingly, we do know a bit about prehistoric shit because of the curious science of archeological coprology. Under certain very special dry conditions, the excrement of our ancestors has become mummified. Probing it with the powerful tools of modern science, researchers have learned about the grains, the meat, and the berries that our ancestors ate, as well as what parasites infected their guts including roundworms (*Ascaris lumbricoides*), whipworms (*Trichuris trichiura*), yokogawa flukes (*Metagonimus yokogawai*), liver flukes (*Clonorchis sinensis*) and beef or pork tapeworms (*Taenia*).[30]

How exactly they cleaned their anuses must, alas, remain a black hole. We can, of course, make an educated guess. Since they were anatomically like us, they suffered the same discomforts that we would suffer having a full butt. Therefore we can surmise that, although they did not have all the wonders of modern anal cleaning technology, they did somehow clean themselves after defecation. Anthropologists stationed in the remote jungles of the world could have told us how so-called primitive tribes performed this necessary act. They certainly were willing to expound freely on the mating habits of the natives, but on this subject they were mainly silent. So we must guess that pre-modern humans would use whatever material was at hand, including their hands—snow in the Arctic, and dirt and leaves in the forest. It is far more difficult for us, with our tender butts, to imagine other products that were reportedly used including wood shavings and sand. But our ancestors were not masochists. The Jorvik Center in York, with exhibits of daily life in prehistoric England, has a lifelike wax figure of a Viking squatting on a latrine. He is holding a nice soft clump of moss in readiness.[31] When moss was not available, they probably used grass or hay. As for other variations on the theme, although we have no direct evidence from the distant past, we do have a few gleanings from the observations of 'primitive' peoples around the world who have yet to be subjected to the 'squeeze the Charmin' television ads.

In 1936, Ernest Stephen an anthropologist visiting the island of Nauru in the middle of the Pacific, made the following observation:

"The pandanus has a composite fruit, something like a giant pineapple. Each separate pandana is broken off and the end chewed while it is twisted round in the mouth to squeeze the juice out. The chewed part is sometimes used as a brush, at other times as toilet paper… There are several varieties of pandanus."[32]

Our nomadic ancestors would use leaves from trees and bushes to wipe themselves, but unlike modern citified folk, they had a much more nuanced understanding of the natural world. Their survival depended on it. These so-called primitive people would not dream of sticking the leaves of any old tree up their rears. Proof of this is that in South Africa there is a tree with the botanical name Peltophorum Africanum and its common name, 'the weeping wattle'. But among local people it has an even more common name; 'the toilet tree.' The wattle is grey green with large feathery leaves that are just perfect for the job.

A guide at Kruger National Park highly recommends the weeping wattle but cautions visitors to carefully brush off all the bugs before insertion. [33]

Sticks and Stones and Water

In the prehistoric world we come across a new category of anal cleansing which may surprise the modern buttocks. To differentiate this group from the wipers and the washers, I call these people, 'the scrapers'. These are people who used some available instrument to scrape the excess feces from their rear ends, very much like a modern plasterer. To people living near the ocean, the ideal instrument would be a clam shell. Its sharp edge and round shape, skillfully deployed, was perfect for the job. The shell of a large nut was used in the same way by those living inland.

Less comfortable and more difficult to use were the round or flat sticks that were in vogue in the Far East. We have archeological proof of this fact: flat sticks called 'chu-gi' recovered in ancient cisterns from the Naru period, 750 CE in Japan.[34]

Sticks were used in this way for thousands of years. We have precise, step-by-step instructions given to Buddhist monks on the method of defecating and subsequent cleaning. The following is from the earliest surviving Buddhist canon (400 BCE), the *Vinaya Pitaka*:

> 1) One should not defecate outside of the cesspool.
>
> 2) While standing outside, one should clear his throat.
>
> 3) Anyone sitting inside should also clear his throat.
>
> 4) Having put aside the (upper) robe on a bamboo pole or a cord, one should enter the place properly and unhurriedly.

5) One shouldn't pull up one's lower robe before entering.

6) One should pull up one's lower robe while standing on the toilet shoes

7) If the place is splattered it should be washed.

8) One should not groan or grunt while defecating.

9) One should not wipe oneself with a rough stick.

10) One should not drop the wiping stick into the cesspool.

11) If the basket for wiping sticks is full, the wiping sticks should be thrown away.

12) One should then cover oneself (with one's lower robe) while standing on the toilet-shoes.

13) One should not leave hurriedly.

14) One should not leave with one's lower robe pulled up

15) One should pull it up while standing on the rinsing-room shoes

16) One shouldn't make a smacking sound while rinsing.

17) One should not leave any water remaining in the rinsing vessel. [35]

It is clear from these instructions that the monks first used a stick to remove the bulk of the feces and then washed their buttocks to finish the job. Note the wise injunction to use only a smooth stick for the first step of the operation. Further research is necessary to understand the admonition not to make a smacking noise while rinsing. It is also clear from the following commentary that the bhikkhus—the ordained monks—were a lot more fastidious about anal cleanliness than the rest of the population (and many of us today).

Now at that time a certain Brahman by birth refused to rinse himself after defecating, thinking, "Who would touch this vile, stinking stuff?" A worm took up residence in his anus. So he told this matter to the bhikkhus. "You mean you don't rinse yourself after defecating?" they asked. "That's right, my friends." Those bhikkhus who were of few wants...criticized and complained and spread it about, "How can a bhikkhu not rinse himself after defecating?" They reported this matter to the Blessed One who said: "If there is water, one should rinse after having defecated. Whoever does not rinse [is committing] an offense of wrong doing."[36]

The Greeks used their hands to wipe their buttocks, specifically their left hand only. In Classical times, there was a superstition about the left. We get the word sinister from the Latin word *sinistra* which originally just meant 'the left side' but later took on a connotation of something evil or unlucky. This could be because only the left hand was assigned to ass wiping activity while only the right hand would be used for such 'clean' activities as picking up one's food or shaking hands with a friend. More sophisticated Greeks, too fancy to handle their own feces, used stones. Thus the familiar Greek proverb:

τρείς είσιν ικανοί πρωκτον απομάξαι λίθοι.
Three stones should be enough to wipe one's ass.

A rare image from a Greek Kylix cir. 500 BCE showing a man using a stone to wipe himself.

In practice, the Greeks used three stones only if they were rough and therefore absorbent; four or more would have to be used, according to authorities in these matters, if the stones were smooth. But the playwright Aristophanes (ca. 446 BCE – ca. 386 BCE) complained that his countrymen were getting soft because:

ἀποψωμεσθα δ' ου λίθοις ἔτι,
ἀλλά σκοροδίοις νπο τρυφης ἑκάστοτε.

We don't even wipe our bottoms with stones any more,
We are so spoilt we now always use garlic cloves!

Which shows that, even back then, there was nostalgia for the good old days. Rich Greeks would also routinely use leeks when in season and men, being the brutes they are, would sometimes use the softest, nearest thing at hand—their togas.

We return to the Romans who launched me on this journey of discovery. They developed a sensible method of both washing and wiping. Here I am again still seated on that ancient Roman toilet at Ephesus:

Two things in this picture give the clue to the Roman method of wiping, the shape of the hole and the channel in front of my feet. Romans used a sponge on a stick—a *xylesphongium*—that they could insert between their legs through the vertical hole and wipe away without having to stand up. These *xylesphongium* were communal sponges. The channel in front would have water flowing through it and the Publiuses and Agrippas of the age would swirl it in the running water after use to make it ready for the next defecator. In less elaborate latrines, the sponges would be sitting in a vase of salt water ready for use and reuse. As the reader will have learned in previous sections of this book, we are in a time long before the discovery of germs, a time long before our own fastidious ideas of what we should and should not share with our fellow human beings.

The stick with the sponge is mentioned in an essay by the Roman philosopher, statesman, and author Lucius Annaeus Seneca. It is in a series entitled *Moral Letters to Lucilius*. The moral of the following horrific story is included in his discussion of when and how a suicide can be honorable:

You need not think that none but great men have had the strength to burst the bonds of human servitude...Nay, men of the meanest lot in life have by a mighty impulse escaped to safety, and when they were not allowed to die at their own convenience, or to suit themselves in their choice of the instruments of death, they have snatched up whatever was lying ready at hand, and by sheer strength have turned objects which were by nature harmless into weapons of their own. For example, there was lately a training-school for gladiators who fight wild beasts in the Forum. A captured German, who was making ready for the morning exhibition, withdrew in order to relieve himself, the only thing which he was allowed to do in secret and without the presence of a guard. While so engaged, he seized the stick of wood, tipped with a sponge, which was devoted to the vilest uses, and stuffed it, just as it was, down his throat; thus he blocked up his windpipe, and choked the breath from his body. That was truly to insult death!

Yes, indeed; it was not a very elegant or becoming way to die; but what is more foolish than to be over-nice about dying? What a brave fellow! He surely deserved to be allowed to choose his fate! How bravely he would have wielded a sword! With what courage he would have hurled himself into the depths of the sea, or down a precipice! Cut off from resources at every hand, yet he found a way to furnish himself with death, and with a weapon for death. Hence you can understand that nothing but the will need postpone death. Let each man judge the deed of this most zealous fellow as he likes, provided we agree on this point; that the foulest death is preferable to the fairest slavery.[37]

Seneca's philosophy was stoicism: a belief in the all-conquering power of the human will.

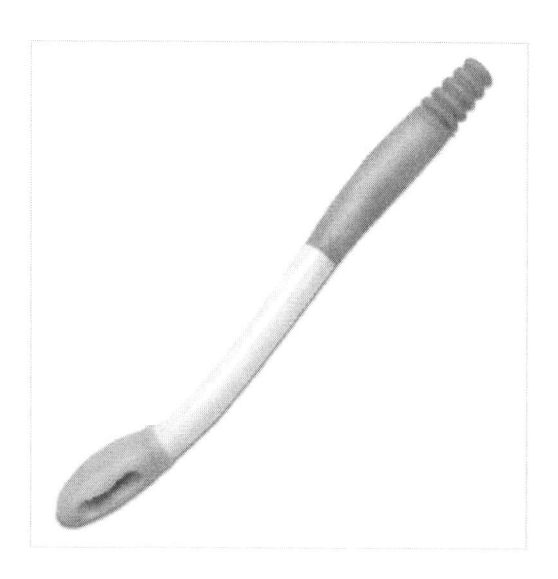

From the sublime to the Internet, the modern incarnation of the Roman spongia on a lignea is called *The Long Reach Comfort Wipe* and is available (Amazon.com, $9.99 plus shipping) for men and women who are too fat to be able to reach their butts. You attach a piece of toilet paper through the slotted hole in the front and wipe. From the tone of the testimonials, the *Long Reach* has been a lifesaver for some.

> I currently weigh 500 lbs and my arm is no longer long enough to reach where it is sometimes needed... I have tried several 'aids' and this is the best by far. Both the handle and the paper ends are covered with what seems to be a type of gripping rubber. This rubber material allows for a secure hand hold as well as a non-slip surface for the paper. The tool is of sufficient width as to give good coverage which may prevent some of the need for multiple attempts. The length is definitely adequate for people in my situation. The tool is curved so that it seems to 'fit' the angles needed for the most comfortable use and positioning. I highly recommend this item for its intended use especially for my large friends.

Meanwhile back in the ancient world, there is some evidence in the literature that the Romans, in spite of their occasional spongings were not very fussy about the cleanliness of their buttocks. The Roman poet Catullus, in graphic terms, praises his friend Furius for his unusually clean rectum:

> *Your body is drier than a horn,*
> *So how can you be otherwise than well and prosperous?*
> *You've no sweat, or phlegm, or snot...*
> *To this cleanliness add an even cleaner one.*
> *That your ass is purer than a little salt-cellar,*
> *And you don't crap more than ten times in a year,*
> *And your shit is harder than beans or pebbles.*
> *So that if you rub it in your hand and crush it,*
> *You can't even dirty your fingers.*[38]

Anal cleansing had been a serious business with the rise of Judaism. The Egyptians believed in absolute purity when dealing with the gods, but now everyone would have to deal with God—a God that sees all. The Jewish Roman historian, Josephus who, as we have seen, had commented on the Egyptian passion for cleanliness, describes, with some astonishment, how the Essenes, an ascetic sect of Jews living around the time of Christ, handled the act of defecation on the day of the Sabbath.

> They are stricter than any other of the Jews in resting from their labors on the seventh day; for they not only get their food ready the day before, that they may not be obliged to kindle a fire on that day, but they will not remove any vessel out of its place, nor go to stool thereon. Nay, some days earlier they have dug a small pit, a foot deep and [on the Sabbath] covering themselves round with their garment, that they may not affront the Divine rays of light, they ease themselves into that pit, after which they put the earth that was dug out again into the pit; and even this they do only in the more lonely places, which they had selected for this purpose. And though this discharge of the excrements is a natural function, they make it a rule to wash themselves after it, as if defiled. [39]

It is clear from Josephus' reaction that this act of washing themselves, including presumably their rear ends, was something he was not used to. In his comment, "though this discharge of the excrements is a natural function," we see a changing attitude towards everything bodily from the hedonistic Roman world to the biblical Jewish world. Shit and shitting no longer is a natural function but rather has become a defilement unless carefully enclosed within religious ritual. The Muslim religion rigorously carried on this tradition.

The founders of Islam continued the ancient Greek tradition of scraping with stones and then washing using the left hand. Anal cleaning is codified in a precise set of does and don'ts. Around 850 AD, the Persian scholar, Sahih Bukhari's (full name Abu Abdullah Muhammad bin Ismail bin Ibrahim bin al-Mughira al-Ja'fai) collected orally transmitted articles of faith in a document called *The Hadith*. Sunni Muslims consider *The Hadith* to be the most authentic and holy book after the Koran. It is here that we find the precise rules for bathroom etiquette including details about anal cleaning that are practiced, with some nod to modernity, by the world's one billion Muslims to this day.

> Allah's Apostle said, "The prayer of a person who is in *Hadath* is not accepted till he performs the ablution." (Note: *Hadath* is the condition of ritual impurity after one passes urine, stool or wind or has had sex.)

> I followed the Prophet while he was going out to answer the call of nature… When I approached near him he said to me, "Fetch for me some stones for ' cleaning the private parts'…So I brought the stones in the corner of my garment and placed them by his side and I then went away from him. When he finished (defecating) he used, them. The Prophet [then] performed ablution by washing the body parts twice. [40]

Stones for the first wipe—and it *must* be an odd (not an even) number of stones—and washing with water to finish the job. Three stones seemed to be the standard, and devout Muslims carried pebbles for this purpose in their turbans.

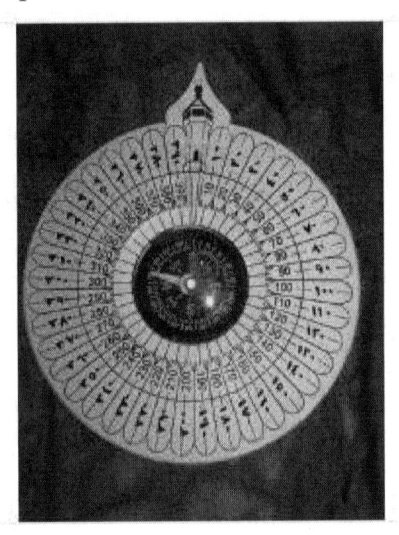

A portable Quibla Compass (to determine the direction of Mecca)

In Islamic Law, specifically the *Taharat* detailing the rules of purity, every aspect of defecation is ritualized. You must enter the toilet area with your left foot; you must not face the direction of Mecca, the sacred direction of prayer, while defecating. (The traveling faithful must therefore carry a compass).

> Aisha, the Prophet's wife says: "I have never seen the Prophet (peace be upon him) coming out after evacuating his bowels without having cleaned himself with water". She spoke to Muslim women and said: "Tell your husbands to clean themselves with water, for I am too shy to tell them so. God's messenger used to do that." [41]

Men are not allowed to chat with a fellow toilet user and are specifically enjoined from touching the other person's penis. You are permitted to touch your own penis but with your left hand only. After defecation, while pouring water from a pitcher, move your left hand from the back of your buttocks towards the front, stopping at the testicles. The reverse direction is not acceptable. (There are no specific wiping instructions for women but presumably they are permitted to wipe in the opposite direction.) The use of the right hand for any of these operations is an abomination. During this action, and while pouring the water and holding the pitcher with your right hand, you must insert a finger (usually the third finger) of your left hand partially into the anal orifice to make sure that it is completely cleaned out. You must do this thrice. If you perform any of these steps incorrectly there is the danger that you will be considered unclean and your prayers will be returned to sender.

Muslims believe that urine is also a substance of impurity and they spend lots of time and effort squeezing and wiping away that last little drop that can lurk at the end of one's penis.

These rituals have changed, of course, with time and technology. Some progressive Imams have even gone as far as declaring the use of toilet paper kosher with the proviso that three sheets are to be used to maintain the sacred tradition. Further, it is written that if your bowel movement was messy. "i.e., the excrement has spread more than normal, if the area dirtied is large... then only water can be used to purify oneself."[42] If a woman's feces is mixed with menstrual blood—a double a'yan najisah or uncleanness— washing is mandatory. It most cases, for the vast majority of Muslim men and women, left-hand cleaning with water alone is the sanctioned and vastly preferred method.

> While praising the people who built Masjid Quba, Allah says, "Therein are men who love to cleanse themselves; and Allah loves those who cleanse themselves" (9:108) When this verse was revealed, the Prophet asked the people of Quba, "What do you do when cleaning yourselves so that Allah will praise you for it?" They said, "We cleanse ourselves with water after emptying the bowels."[43]

The early Christian saints, as we have seen, considered washing to be somewhat decadent. With their thoughts fixed firmly on their eternal souls, they left their butts to take care of themselves. In Europe in the Middle Ages, those who could afford it used cloth to wipe themselves—used, and reused the same cloth. We have documentary proof of this. Old latrines are a gold mine for archeologists because in digging through these sites they get valuable clues to how people actually lived.

Examining the middens under the well-ordered latrines of medieval monasteries, these diligent researchers have found very worn strips of rough woolen cloth. After the habits of the monks and nuns became too threadbare they were cut up for toilet use and reuse and, when the cloth became too holey and tattered for even this purpose, it went down the hole. To keep their bathroom practices secret from the laity, the monks even created a code word for this material: *anitergium* combining the Latin *ani,* anus, with *tergeo,* to wipe off. In the same latrines researchers found buckhorn seeds, a common remedy for constipation brought on, perhaps, by many hours spent immobile in earnest prayer.

The elite of the period wore much softer clothing—fine linen and cotton—which became much softer rags to be used to wipe their elite asses, but not very thoroughly according to one 12th century author:

> We see some people who, although they are carefully brought up, well versed in the sciences and knowledgeable about the world, nevertheless have a certain decided taste for shit. This liking for shit is so strong that they always carry a little bit around with them. Not in vases of course, but a little on the tails of their shirts and on their clothing.[44]

Not all of the nobility used linen on or off their shirts to wipe their asses. In the expense account of the Duc de Berry in 1400 we find an order for four pounds of *étoupe*—course fibers of flax or hemp not yet wound into ropes—which he seemed to prefer for his manlier butt. Chacun à son gout.

> *What am I seeing oh God!*
> *It is night soil.*
> *What a wonderful substance it is.*
> *It is excreted by even the greatest of kings*
> *Its odor speaks of majesty.*
>
> Alexis Piron (1689-1773)

F. Scott Fitzgerald once quipped that the rich are different from you and me. That certainly is true when it comes to the behinds of the Kings of England. In the early years of his reign, Henry VIII appointed the sons of noblemen to act as his personal secretaries, carrying out a variety of administrative tasks within his private chambers. The most honored and intimate of these appointments had the formal title, 'Groom of the King's Close-Stool'. The close-stool, you will remember, is the box with a chamber pot in it. The duty of this lucky appointee was to wipe the royal ass. As strange as it might seem to us, this position was not considered at all demeaning. Quite the contrary, the position was an especially prized one, because he who had access to the King's rear also had access to the King's ear. In 1521, Sir William Brereton got the job of keeping Henry's "house of easement sweet and clear" and thus being so close to the seat of power, Brereton rose to a position of enormous influence and wealth. He was feared and respected by everyone at court until 1536 when he took the wrong side of a royal dispute and got his noble head chopped off.

This tradition was carried on by Elizabeth the First. The wiping duties of her attendants were the same, but she at least changed the name of the office to the more elegant 'First Lady of the Bedchamber'. This royal appointment continued until 1901 with its named bizarrely changed to 'Groom of the Stole'. The title became purely honorific because we may assume that later British monarchs learned how to wipe their own behinds.

The French Monarchs, not to be outwiped, had a royal appointment: *Le Porte-Coton*—the carrier of cotton, which gives us a clue of the material this courtier used to perform his royal office. This office existed well into the 19th century, as seen in this elegant sketch by the court artist Horace Vernet immortalizing the bowel movement and subsequent wiping of King Louis XVIII on December 20, 1816.

England's James I (1566-1625) was not even elegant enough to lower his trousers. The courtier Sir Roger L'Estrange described how he was so passionate about hunting that he would ride all day never dismounting to go to the necessary. When he returned home at night his attendants had the job of pulling him out of his soiled clothing and wiping up the mess.

Having someone else wipe your ass was not the exclusive domain of Western kings. In China certain mandarins cultivated enormous long fingernails – a foot or more in length and sheathed them in jade or ivory except for moments of formal display. Such nails were public announcements that the man always had servants to clean his anus. [45]

The Japanese military dictators—the Shoguns—who ruled Japan from the 17th century, had two servants in attendance during elimination, one to fan him and the other to wipe.

As we have seen, Brahmins of India were obliged to keep their rectums scrupulously clean. In the state of Mysore well into the 19th century it was the task of their dutiful wives to wash their high-caste tuchuses.

Ordinary mortals, of course, were reduced to performing this office for themselves. Unfortunately, as is usual in historical surveys of all kinds, we have very little hard information about exactly how, and with what, the common folk did it. We must remind ourselves that before the Industrial Revolution and the era of mass production and easy transportation, material goods of all kinds were laboriously made by hand and were very precious. A piece of cloth, even an old and used piece of cloth, was an asset. Cloth of any sort would have been a great luxury for the peasantry, who would consider themselves fortunate to own an extra shirt. One would like to think that they too would have enjoyed the use of fabric, but given their lives spent mainly in the fields of the master scratching out a meager living, grass or hay or leaves would be the likely medium that they used to scratch their rear ends after defecation. In season, however, they could enjoy the broad leaves of the ever-present chestnut tree.

As France's peasants slowly starved to death in the 17th and 18th centuries and the nobility rose to obscene heights of wretched excess, a debate raged in the salons between those who preferred satin and those who used velvet to *torche cul* (to wipe ass). The poet Eustorg de Beaulieu favored the latter.

Du velours vaut mieux que de satin,
Pour torcher son cul au matin.

No mere velvet for the second wife of Louis XVI. Mme de Maintenon used only the ultra-soft wool from Merino sheep. Not to be one-upped in this matter, Louis XV's mistress, Madame de Pompadour, would only allow fine lace to touch her tail.

The working man and woman continued to use whatever was at hand well into the 19th century. People living near the ocean followed the tradition of scraping, using shells into modern times. Samuel Rolleston gives this report of a surprised English traveler using a communal latrine in Holland when "an old woman set herself on the next hole to the gentleman and civilly offered him her mussel shell by way of scraper after she had done herself."[46]

Outhouses throughout the rural American West were provided with an unusual wiping device—corncobs. They would be supplied either in boxes or hanging from a nail on the wall, presumably for use and re-use. They would be plentiful on the farm—nicely absorbent, relatively soft (except in winter), and biodegradable when dropped down the hole of the cesspit.

19th Century child's potty. Note the receptacle for the corncobs on the lid.

Proof that there are no absolutes when it comes to either toilets or wiping is the nostalgic fondness that many people expressed for the defecation rituals of their youth no matter how rough. We see this in a touching doggerel, 'The Old Backhouse,' by the Hoosier poet, James Witcomb Riley (1849-1916):

When memory keeps me company and moves to smiles or tears,
A weather-beaten object looms through the mist of years.
Behind the house and barn it stood, a hundred yards or more,
And hurrying feet a path had made, straight to its swinging door.
When the crust was on the snow and the sullen skies were gray.
In sooth the building was no place where one could wish to stay.
We did our duties promptly, there one purpose swayed the mind;

We tarried not, nor lingered long on what we left behind.
The torture of that icy seat would make a Spartan sob,
For need must scrape the goose flesh with a lacerating cob,
That from a frost-encrusted nail, was suspended by a string
For father was a frugal man and wasted not a thing...

I began this survey bemoaning the paucity of fiction on the subject of anal cleansing. The act was either too commonplace or too repulsive to ever become the subject of literature ancient or modern. There is however one exception. It comes from the ribald pen of a French ex-monk; François Rabelais. Born near the end of the 15th century, Rabelais was an authentic version of that overused phrase—a Renaissance man.

He was a practicing physician, an editor of classical Latin texts, and an author. He used the medium of humor and satire to attack the rigid establishment authorities of his time and put forward his own belief in humanism and individual liberty. In his major work, *Gargantua and Pantagruel,* he imagines a free-for-all Abbey of Thélème that both satirizes the loose morals of the monasteries of the day and envisions an institution with drinking, feasting, sex, and the wild exercise of free will that would make even a modern-day hippy communard blush. Rabelais sets out to shock and his vivid, grotesque descriptions of bodily functions can even make today's jaded jaws drop.

The reason Rabelais comes into our story is that, included in the extra-ordinary adventures of the heroes of his epic, is an entire chapter on the subject of ass wiping. It occurs in a description of the education of the young giant Gargantua, in which Gargantua describes to his father, Grangousier, his inventive experimentation with every imaginable and (a few unimaginable) methods of *torche cul* (ass wiping). In the English edition of Rabelais' works published in 1898, the Victorian editor described the chapter you are about to read as "most un-fragrant and undesirable" and he refused to translate it. He did however print it uncut in all its antique French language glory.

It is, of course, meant to be humorous but, like all humor, there is within this extraordinary text a few clues as what materials people actually used in the late Middle Ages to perform that most unfragrant of acts.

Gargantua and Pantagruel, Book One Chapter 13 [47]

About the end of the fifth year, Grangousier returning from the conquest of the Canarians, went by the way to see his son Gargantua. There he was filled with joy at the sight of such a child as his. And whilst he kissed and embraced him, he asked many childish questions of him about divers matters, and drank very freely with him and with his governesses, of whom in great earnest he asked, amongst other things, whether they had been careful to keep him clean and sweet. To this Gargantua answered, that he had taken such a course for that himself, that in all the country there was not to be found a cleanlier boy than he. How is that? said Grangousier. "I have," answered Gargantua, "by a long and curious experience, found out a means to wipe my bum, the most lordly, the most excellent, and the most convenient that ever was seen." "What is that?" said Grangousier, "how is it?" "I will tell you by-and-by," said Gargantua. "Once I wiped me with a gentle-woman's velvet mask, and found it to be good; for the softness of the silk was very voluptuous and pleasant to my fundament. Another time with one of their hoods, and in a like manner that was comfortable. At another time with a lady's neckerchief, and after that I wiped me with some ear-pieces of hers made of crimson satin, but there were so many golden spangles in them (damn round things—a pox take them) that they ripped away all the skin of my ass with a vengeance. (Now I wish St. Antony's fire would burn the ass of the goldsmith that made them, and of her that wore them!) This hurt I cured by wiping myself with a page's cap, garnished with a feather in the fashion of the caps worn by the Swiss Guards.

Afterwards, in shitting behind a bush, I found a cat and I wiped my breech with it but her claws were so sharp that they scratched and ulcerated my perineum. I recovered from this the next morning by wiping myself with my mother's gloves, of a most excellent perfume and scent of the Arabian Benin. After that I wiped me with sage, with fennel, with anet, with marjoram, with roses, with gourd-leaves, with beets, with colewort, with leaves of the vine-tree, with mallows, wool-blade, which is a tail-scarlet, with lettuce, and with spinach leaves. All this did very great good to my leg. Then with a dog's mercury plant, with parsley, with nettles, and with comfrey, but that gave me bloody diarrhea, which I healed by wiping myself with the codpiece of my trousers. Then I wiped my tail in the sheets, in the coverlet, in the curtains, with a cushion, with a tapestry hanging, with a green carpet, with a table-cloth, with a napkin, with a handkerchief, with a combing-cloth; in all of which I found more pleasure than do the mangy dogs when you rub them."

"Yes," said Grangousier, "but which ass wipe did you find to be the best?" "I'm coming to it," said Gargantua, "and by-and-by shall you hear the tu autem, and know the whole mystery and knot of the matter. I wiped myself with hay, with straw, with thatch-rushes, with flax, with wool, with paper, but,

> Who fouls his ass with a paper wipe,
> Shall on his balls leave some blight…"

Said Grangousier., "Pray, go on in this torcheculative, or wipe-bummatory discourse…" "Afterwards I wiped my bum," said Gargantua, "with a handkerchief, with a pillow, with a slipper, with a pouch, with a basket, but that was a wicked and unpleasant ass wipe; then with a hat. Of hats, note that some are shorn, and others shaggy, some velvet, others covered with taffetas, and others with satin. The best of all these is the shaggy hat, for it makes a very neat absorption of the fecal matter.

Afterwards I wiped my tail with a hen, with a cock, with a pullet, with a calf's skin, with a hare, with a pigeon, with a cormorant, with an attorney's bag, with a hunter's cap, with a nun's cap, with a falconer's lure. But, to conclude, I say and maintain that of all torcheculs, arsewipes, bumfodders, tail-napkins, bunghole cleansers, and wipe-breeches, there is none in the world comparable to the neck of a goose that is well downed, if you hold her head betwixt your legs. And believe me therein upon mine honor, for you will thereby feel in your rear a most wonderful pleasure, both in regard of the softness of the said down and of the temperate heat of the goose, which is easily communicated to the ass hole and the rest of the inwards, in so far as to come even to the regions of the heart and brains. And think not that the felicity of the heroes and demigods in the Elysian Fields consists neither in their immortal flowers, ambrosia, nor nectar but in this, according to my judgment; that they wipe their tails with the neck of a goose, holding her head betwixt their legs."

In this encyclopedia of late medieval anal cleansing, we have a climax with the image of a wipe of a greater softness, absorbency, and warmth than was ever dreamed up in the most creative advertising copywriter's mind. Note that in the middle of this outpouring, the child giant soundly rejects the use of paper wipes, 'papier torche' in the French original, as being particularly disgusting because the paper left a bit of shit on his testicles. Although he scorned it, this is perhaps the first reference in modern Western literature to the use of paper as a medium of wiping. Which gives us a perfect segue to the next station of our exotic journey.

PAPER!

The Chinese invented paper probably before the time of Christ. All paper is manufactured by pounding vegetable or textile material until it becomes a slurry in water. The suspended mass is pressed onto a screen and the water is allowed to drain away. When dry, the resulting thin layer of intertwined fibers is what we call paper. Until the mid-19th century, all paper was made by hand. We know it as that remarkable medium on which we can record financial records, religious edicts, mathematical formulae, and shopping lists so that we can transport this information through time and space. Along with electricity, the telephone, and the computer, paper was an invention that fundamentally transformed human life.

Early Chinese paper was heavy and fibrous, something like blotting paper, if anyone remembers that exotic substance today. This paper did not at first replace the traditional Chinese writing material, which consisted of thin slabs made from bamboo and other wood. It certainly was not used for printing, a technology that was invented hundreds of years later. Paper was first used in China to wrap food and medicine and to pack delicate objects such as pottery and mirrors for transportation over bumpy roads. It was also used to make fans, lanterns, kites, translucent windows and for use in the toilet.

There is no need to explain why paper is a wonderful substance for this purpose. It is thin, soft, absorbent, relatively cheap, and easily disposable. What a pleasant advance over grass, sand, or that expensive cloth or sponge which one would have to wash and reuse.

We have quite a bit of documentary evidence that the Chinese used their wonderful invention for this purpose. And not just any old paper. The scholar Yen Chih-Thui (531-591 AD) wrote instructions to his family that "Paper on which there are quotations from the Five Classics (the religious books of Confucianism) or the names of the sages, I dare not use for toilet purposes."[48] We also have reports like this one from a rather disgusted Muslim traveler around 800 AD who, as we have seen, was required by his faith to wash his buttocks thoroughly after defecation. The Chinese, he complained, "are not careful about cleanliness and they do not wash themselves with water when they have done their necessities; but they only wipe themselves with paper."[49]

'Tshao chih' 草紙 was the special grade of paper which the Chinese manufactured to be used for wiping. Made from the tender fiber of the plentiful rice straw and requiring less labor to produce than writing paper, it was therefore inexpensive. Like today's bathroom tissue, huge quantities were made. We know this because, like any good bureaucracy, the Imperial Court kept meticulous records. In the year 1393 alone 720,000 sheets of *tshao chih* was manufactured for use by the court—the size, approximately two by three feet, presumably to be cut up into smaller squares by the users. The imperial rectums, here as elsewhere, got special attention. For them, a special paper was manufactured: light yellow, thick but soft, and perfumed, of course. So much rice straw (and lime to dissolve it into a slurry) was needed to manufacture the paper to keep the asses of Chinese royalty wiped that the Imperial Paper Factory always had a huge mound of this raw material on its grounds, affectionately dubbed the Elephant Mountain. And it was not only royalty that had the luxury of using paper to wipe. Joseph Needham, the historian of Chinese science and technology, quotes statistics to show that billions of sheets of toilet paper were manufactured by factories all over China well into the 20th century.

During these two thousand years or so, Europeans continued to wipe their butts with anything at hand, and for most of this period the rest of their anatomy was none too clean. It is no wonder that the Chinese looked on visiting Westerners as barbarians. It took many years for Europe to emerge from this backside backwardness, and use paper instead of more abrasive materials.

The Romans did have a paper-like material. When they wished to write down their thoughts on something a little more portable than stone tablets, they used papyrus, a thin material stripped from the stem of a plant of the same name. Thicker and not as flexible as paper, it nevertheless served its purpose and another purpose according to the Roman satirical poet Gaius Valerius Catullus. In his poem number 36, he wrote that his lover promised to burn in sacrifice to the gods "writings of the worst poet" in Rome, if he would return to her arms. Catullus mischievously selects the popular poet Volusis for this honor and begins this strange love poem with the lines:

Annales Volusi, cacata carta,
Uotum soluite pro mea puella.
The chronicles of Volusis, shit encrusted paper
Have discharged the vow of my sweetheart.

The onomatopoeic phrase *'cacata carta'* indicates that the works of poor old forgotten Volusis must have done toilet duty in the latrines of Rome when the sponges on a stick were otherwise occupied.

Although the dictionary translates the word 'carta' as paper, the Romans were still using papyrus. In fact it took well over a thousand years for the Chinese invention of paper to make its way to Europe. Serious manufacture of the product in the West began only with the implementation in the 15th century of that other great Chinese invention—printing.

Books, at first, were very expensive and rare but the thin absorbent stuff on which they were impressed was just too tempting to resist for use as what would later be called bumf (short for bum fodder). As we have seen in the 17th century poem at the head of this book:

…Physick, music, and poetry,
Now to no other purpose tend,
But to defend the fingers' end

This usage was feared by authors who were appalled to discover that their printed words of wisdom—their tickets to immortality—were disappearing down the guardrobes, chamber pots, and cesspits of the time. There are reports that some authors were so paranoid about this possibility that they would only release their works printed on vellum, a heavy leather-like material very unsuitable for wiping. This was a method chosen by religious authorities who were extremely upset that the word of God might end up up somebody's anus.

Of course it depends on whose God. As seen in Catullus' poem, ass wiping can be used as the supreme expression of contempt. Contempt was no more in evidence than in the 16th century during the bitter blood feud between Protestants and Catholics for European domination. The German priest Martin Luther, the leader of the Protestant Reformation movement, told his followers that, "we may with a good conscience take [the Pope's] coat-of-arms…to the privy, use them for wiping and then throw them in the fire. It would be even better if it was the Pope himself." This, he suggested, should be done for the "glory of God." On a similarly high intellectual plane of theological discourse, Thomas More, the British lawyer and Catholic polemicist, answered Luther: "Since he has written that he already has a prior right to bespatter and besmirch the royal crown with shit, will we not have the posterior right to proclaim the beshitted tongue of this practitioner of posterioristics most fit to lick the very posterior of a pissing female mule."[50]

This metaphorical ass wiping became actual when the British embraced Protestantism in the 16th century. During this period, the property of the Catholic Church was confiscated and individuals came into possession of many monasteries with their extensive libraries of religious tracts. John Bale, (1495-1563) an ally of Thomas Cromwell and hater of Catholics, recorded with some glee what happened to these ancient manuscripts:

> A great nombre of them whych purchased those superstycyous mansyons, reserued of those lybrarye bokes, some to serue theyr jakes [toilets], some to scoure theyr candelstyckes, and some to rubbe their bootes.[51]

Among the believers, the symbolic power of words printed on paper is as explosive an issue today as it was 500 hundred years ago.

Zee News
Tuesday, April 19, 2011

Kabul: Three people have been arrested as officials probe claims that a paper mill in Afghanistan recycled copies of the Quran into toilet paper, the attorney general's office said Tuesday. Around 1,000 angry demonstrators, some throwing stones, held a protest yesterday at the mill on the outskirts of Kabul, leaving the building partially destroyed. Copies of the Quran were found inside the factory, Kabul police spokesman Hashmat Stanikzai said, adding that no-one was injured in the protest. "The attorney general's office and Kabul police have jointly tasked a delegation to investigate the alleged disrespect to our holy book in that factory," a spokesman for the office, Amanullah Iman said. "We have arrested three people including the director of the company so far... we are taking the issue very seriously."

Meanwhile back in the Middle Ages, some writers of the time bad-mouthed the use of paper for wiping, not for theological reasons, but simply because, compared to lambs wool or linen, the book paper of the day didn't do its job very well. Opined one French author, "instead of taking away the crap it just flattens and plasters the stuff." (*Il ne font qu'aplatire et replâtrer les matières.*) "Worse," he wrote, "sometimes the paper breaks and you end up with a finger up your hole."[52]

But in spite of these cavils, the general population knew when they had a good thing up their ass. In the 18th century, as books became commonplace, many had a second life in the chamber pots of Europe and America. All the various varieties of printed ephemera such as pamphlets and newspapers, were on the way to becoming the wipe of choice; much to the loss of future cultural historians. There were even complaints to the postal authorities that some letters reached this unfortunate destination because of mailmen in dire need.

In 1753, the printer J. Lewis decided to go with the flow and published a work of doggerel verse in the form of a loosely bound folio entitled: *Bum-Fodder for the Ladies: a Poem upon soft paper,* price, 6 pence. Not surprisingly, the soft-paper editions of this book have become an extreme rarity. The work is available on microfilm from CT Research Publications, Inc.[53] (which seems to defeat its true purpose). The magazine, *The Monthly Review* panned the literary quality of the work calling it "impudent and illiterate nonsense!"

L'ART DE CHIER,

POËME,

PAR ARGAUD DEBARGES.

A PARIS,

Chez DROST aîné, rue Neuve-Notre-Dame,
Et chez les Marchands de Nouveautés.

1806.

In his epic 1806 poem *L'art de chier* (The Art of Shitting) Argand Debarges, writes that he sells this work for six sou and:

Quand il aura bien lu et relu mon cahier,
Il pourra s'en servir s'il manqué de papier.

When you've read and re-read my little book, you can (still) make use of it if there is a lack of paper.

Philip Dormer Stanhope, the 4th Earl of Chesterfield (1694-1773) was a politician and brilliant essayist. In the mid-eighteenth century he wrote a series of letters to his son, then away at school, advising him on the ways of the world. After Chesterfield's death, his son's widow published these letters in book form and it became a best seller because it taught middle-class wannabes upper-class manners. Lord Chesterfield was the father that every son dreads, a stern taskmaster exhorting the kid to use every second of the day to promote his betterment. He enters our story because of letter number 133 written on December 11, 1747:

> Dear Boy,
>
> There is nothing which I more wish that you should know, and which fewer people do know, than the true use and value of time. It is in every body's mouth; but in few people's practice...
>
> I knew a gentleman, who was so good a manager of his time, that he would not even lose that small portion of it, which the

calls of nature obliged him to pass in the necessary-house; but gradually went through all the Latin poets, in those moments. He bought, for example, a common edition of Horace, of which he tore off gradually a couple of pages, carried them with him to that necessary place, read them first, and then sent them down as a sacrifice to Cloacina: [i.e. the sewer] this was so much time fairly gained; and I recommend to you to follow his example. It is better than only doing what you cannot help doing at those moments; and it will make any book, which you shall read in that manner, very present in your mind. Books of science, and of a grave sort, must be read with continuity; but there are very many, and even very useful ones, which may be read with advantage in snatches, and unconnectedly; such are all the good Latin poets, (except Virgil in his Aeneid): and such are most of the modern poets, in which you will find many pieces worth reading, that will not take up above seven or eight minutes.

Chesterfield also recommended the English dictionary for the poor boy to peruse as being ideal episodic reading material. He advised his son to avoid reading the writings of the poet Virgil while on the toilet. These can only be digested in continuity, he warned, and must not be started and stopped with the diurnal call of nature.

> *There was a young fellow named Chivy*
> *Who, whenever he went to the privy,*
> *First solaced his mind,*
> *Then wiped his behind,*
> *With some well-chose pages of Livy.*
> *Anon. limerick*

This was neither the first nor the last debate about the exact nature of the printed matter to be inserted between the cheeks of one's buttocks. In the late 18th century, loyal comrades of the atheistic French Revolution were convinced that the pages of religious writings, now freely available in French lavatories, were giving them constipation, a condition that was only cured, so they claimed, after they were supplied with printed material having the correct ideological slant.

Along with the printed ephemera, many a priceless masterpiece was 'sacrificed to cloacina'. One wonders how many Shakespeare plays, Milton poems, and Bach cantatas suffered a similar fate. The book collector W. Carew Hazlitt reports that one sharp-eyed bibliophile found, hanging on the wall of a lavatory at Harrogate, this now priceless 1474 edition of the History of Troy, the first book printed in England.

This unfortunate story is proof, if proof is needed, that there was a great demand for paper of all kinds—a demand that was becoming a crisis in the 19th century. Until the 1800s, as we have seen, all paper was hand-made and in the West it was made from old rags. The process was slow and labor-intensive and, with need for more and more paper by the publishing industry, raw materials were in short supply.

Two inventions changed this situation. In England, the Fourdrinier brothers perfected a machine that could produce huge

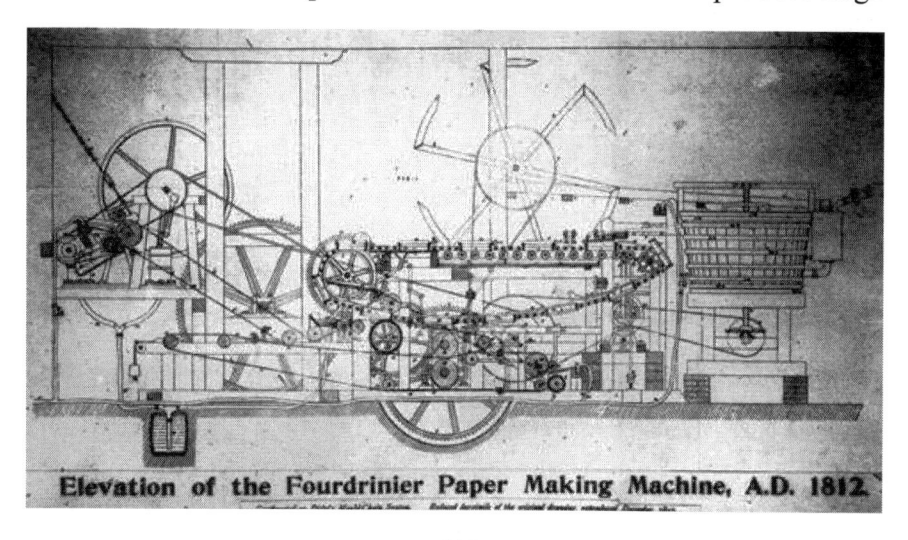

Elevation of the Fourdrinier Paper Making Machine, A.D. 1812

rolls of paper continuously on an industrial scale. In Canada, Charles Fenerty developed a way of chemically treating wood chips and processing them into a pulp suitable for the manufacture of paper. By mid-century huge quantities were rolling out of the paper mills of the western world. Newspapers were transformed from small densely-printed folio sheets into the multi-page large format editions that we know today.

There was no longer any question of what Westerners would use in the privy. Now even the most impoverished citizen had access to a plentiful supply of this modern wiping wonder. When you went into a public lavatory, the attendant would hand you paper neatly cut up into squares after you paid your customary penny. At home, indoor water closets were supplied with small boxes to hold the cut up paper. In outhouses, all through the 19th and 20th centuries, across America you would find the famous Sears catalogue hanging on a nail. Multi-paged and just the right size, it provided the ideal episodic reading that Lord Chesterfield praised and, because a fresh catalogue would be mailed every spring, there was no regret about sending its richly illustrated pages down the hole. One writer reported however, that before allowing it in the family outhouse, his mother would go through the catalogue ripping out all the pages showing images of women's undergarments so that naughty boys would get no inspiration while in the privacy of the privy.

The use of the catalogues all through the farmlands of Middle America was so prevalent into the 1940s that businessmen from the city referred to it as 'the cob and catalog belt'. It is reported that when, in the 1940s, Sears started printing their catalogue on shiny coated paper to better illustrate their wares, they received hundreds of letters of complaint from irate consumers.

In Germany's hyperinflation of the 1920s, banknotes were printed by the millions on nice thin paper. Having the perfect size and texture, they were still in use in German bathrooms into the 1960s.

Zimbabwe recently went through a similar bout of hyper-inflation and their once-proud currency suffered the same inglorious fate causing sewage problems across the continent.

As late as the 1950s, in cafes across Europe you would still find magazines hanging on hooks or nails by the squat toilets. In working-class neighborhoods of Paris patrons were said to prefer *'Le Petite Echo de la Mode'* an upscale fashion magazine, while in countryside loos there was the ubiquitous *'Le Chasseur Français.'*

Of course, when certain writings are used in this way, a wipe is not just a wipe. In James Joyce's *Ulysses,* we have an extremely detailed description of Leopold Bloom taking a crap while reading about the results of a poetry-writing contest in the daily newspaper. As is Joyce's genius, he describes the scene with layers of overlapping meanings. "Quietly he read, restraining himself, the first column and yielding but resisting, began the second." The published poem winning a prize of three and a half pounds makes Bloom a bit jealous so after peeing and dreaming in a stream of consciousness he

> tore way half the prize story sharply and wiped himself with it. Then he girded up his trousers... pulled back the jerky shaky door of the jakes [i.e. the bathroom] and came forth from the gloom into the air.

A similarly poetic response to a newspaper is expressed in a letter from a touchy German composer, Johann Reger (1873-1916), to a critic:"*Ich sitze in dem kleinsten Zimmer in meinem Hause. Ich habe ihre Kritik vor mir. Im nachsten Augenblick wird sie hinter mir sein!*" "I am sitting in the smallest room of my house. I have your review before me. In a moment it will be behind me!"

With reams of free paper available to everyone, used once and then quickly dropped in the pot, the obvious question must be asked; why would anyone in his or her right mind spend good money to buy a specially made product soon to be called toilet paper? The answer requires an excursion into the confluence of business history and the technology of the toilet.

We don't know much about the New York business man Joseph C. Gayetty, but he was a true pioneer. In 1857, he was the first person in the Western world to manufacture and market a product that he called 'paper for the water closet'. And why spend 50 cents (a lot of money in those days) for his product rather than the sports section of the Daily News? Mr. Gayetty explained why his invention was; "The Greatest Necessity of the Age!"

> ### *The Greatest Necessity of the Age!*
> # GAYETTY'S
> ## Medicated Paper,
> ### FOR THE WATER-CLOSET.
>
> **Read and Learn What is in Ordinary Paper.**
>
> MANY people have wooed their own destruction, physical and mental, by neglecting to pay attention to ordinary matters. Few persons would believe that a beautiful enameled card contains a quantum of arsenic, with other chemicals, which, if used to any extent, will communicate poison, and that fatally. All printing or writing papers contain either Oil of Vitriol, Chloride of Lime, Potash, Soda Ash, White Clay, Lime, Ultramine or OXALIC ACID. White paper contains either some or all of these fearful poisons, while colored papers, (excepting GAYETTY's, which is a pearl color, and made to be as pure as snow,) embody portions of Prussiate of Potash, Bichromate of Potash, Muriatic Acid, Prussian Blue, Aqua-Fortis, Copperas, and a variety of other articles equally dangerous and pernicious, but too numerous to be catalogued in our little circular. Physicians owe it to the rising generation to caution all against touching or tasting such deleterious and death-dealing material. Printed paper, everybody knows is rank poison to tender portions of the body. Individuals would not put printers ink in their mouths, as one of its ingredients is LAMP BLACK—yet they have no hesitation in allowing themselves and children to lay in a plentiful crop of piles—or aggravating them if they exist—by applying that ink to the tenderest part of the body corporate, if we except the eye. How much cheaper in every respect is it to use a paper made of the purest material and medicated with the greatest care. Such is GAYETTY's MEDICATED PAPER. For sale by
>
> ### J. RUSSELL SPALDING,
> ### 27 Tremont Street, Boston.
>
> Look for the inventor's name water-marked in each sheet of the genuine, thus:
>
> # J C GAYETTY
> # N Y
>
> BARTON & SON Print, 111 Fulton street.

By using newspaper to wipe, he warned, you are applying ink, lamp black, oxalic acid, oil of vitriol, and other poisons "equally dangerous and pernicious but too numerous to be catalogued in our little circular to the tenderest part of the body corporate." Who knew that they were 'wooing our own destruction' in this way?

Gayetty followed up his circulars with a series of newspaper ads detailing the exact nature of this destruction:

The print is crude, the reproduction from old microfilm poor, but here it is, right above the port wine, one man's attempt to change the bathroom habits of the western world.

> has snatched from death. Nothing equal to it. For sale by Dr. S. B. SMITH, 322 Canal street, near Church, and by G. C. Wells & Co., 115 Franklin street.
>
> NEW AND EXCELLENT.—SO FAR AS THE AFFLICtive and dangerous disease called the piles is concerned, the physicians are likely to be cheated of their fees. Mr. J. C. GAYETTY, an experienced paper maker, has succeeded in producing a medicated paper, which not only cures, but prevents piles, if used systematically in the water closet. This paper is put up in packages of 500 to 1,000 sheets, which are sold at 50 cents and $1 the package; less even than the price given for ordinary poisonous and pile-producing waste paper. The matter is really worth the attention of all persons who desire to be sound in health and cleanly in habits. Sold by the single package, or at wholesale, by J. C. GAYETTY, No. 41 Ann street.
>
> PORT WINE, BOTTLED IN PORTUGAL.
> In consequence of the extreme difficulty generally experienced in all parts of the United States, of procuring in all its native purity and excellence,
> GENUINE PORT WINE

Despite the claim by Mr. Gayetty and hundreds of subsequent ads, 'ordinary poisonous paper' cannot, in fact, be 'pile-producing'. Half of the entire human race suffers from hemorrhoids (commonly called piles) sometime in their lives, (another argument along with our fragile backs, against intelligent design). Hemorrhoids occur when the veins in the anal canal become swollen and they are a common side effect of pregnancy. They are not life-threatening but can be terribly itchy and/or horribly painful. Rectal bleeding will occur if the enlarged veins are ruptured. Mr. Gayetty is correct to the extent that constant rubbing with hard newspaper can, in fact, irritate the delicate perineum area around the anus and exacerbate the existing condition.

Another cause of piles, according to doctors, is sitting too long on the toilet while reading said newspaper.

Gayetty was offering a paper impregnated with a soothing oil, perhaps aloe, and promises that 50 cents will bring not only posterior relief but also revenge by 'cheating the physicians of their fees.' There is no way of telling whether the next ad appearing in the *New York Herald* a few weeks later on December 10, 1858 was just advertising hype or whether his water closet paper was really flying off the shelf.

> GAYETTY'S MEDICATED PAPER FOR THE WATER closet, was comparatively unknown four weeks ago; it is now used by everybody that appreciates health and cleanliness. As a cure for the piles it will take the place of all vaunted nostrums that destroy the system; and as a preventive it cannot be too highly appreciated. It should especially be placed in every "lady's toilet." Recollect that all other paper, whether white, colored or printed, produces and aggravates piles. Depot 41 Ann street. For sale by all respectable druggists: by Mrs. Hayes, of Fulton street, Brooklyn, and Callender & Co., Philadelphia.
> N. B.—J. C. Gayetty, N. Y., is watermarked in each sheet.

What is significant here is Gayetty's implication that the paper has a more universal application than just treating piles. He states that it is "now used by everybody that appreciated health and cleanliness" and that "it should especially be placed in every lady's toilet (i.e. dressing table)." This is the first reference in print associating the paper with the word 'toilet' a word that, because of Gayetty's creative advertising copy, was soon to become the name given to the object into which we poop.

It is obvious that Gayetty had hit on something profitable because soon after his product's introduction and, for the next ten years, Gayetty's ads were complaining of evil toilet paper counterfeiters:

> JUNE 21, 1869.   H. H. UPHAM, 290 Broadway, Metal Sign Manufacturer.
>
> GAYETTY'S MEDICATED PAPER.—BEWARE OF poisonous imitations. The great popularity and usefulness of this paper has induced some unscrupulous persons to manufacture a poisonous counterfeit which it is dangerous to use. Genuine has water mark of J. C. Gayetty, New York, on each sheet; 50 cents per package. Wholesale and retail at JOHN F. HENRY'S United States Family Medicine Warehouse, No. 8 College place, New York.

It is also clear that after 1857, Americans had a new product in their hands and some were willing to pay for it. Soon paper manufacturers in America and England jumped on Gayetty's bandwagon, turning out nice thin paper packaged in sheets, without even the fiction that it is for piles. I can authoritatively report that one brand came in 5 x 7 inch sheets, is beige in color, and has the consistency of tissue paper. I know this because I located and purchased a package of this ephemera of ephemera on Ebay. The copy on the package states that "Bromo has been on the market since 1872 and is known in most civilized countries." By that time, poor Gayetty had many competitors, reminding us that it isn't only in the high-tech world that the innovators can ultimately be the losers.

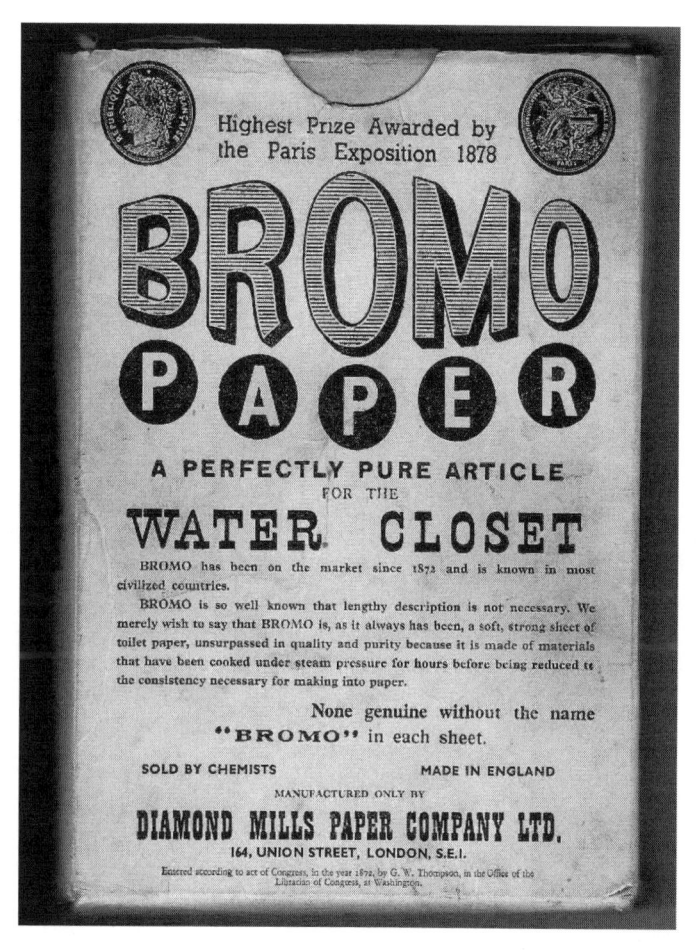

Whoever thought up the term 'toilet paper' was probably inspired by Gayetty's ad suggesting that the product had a place on every 'lady's toilet'. Remember that in the 19th century the word 'toilet' referred *only* to personal grooming and grooming activities and not to that object that dares not speak its name. (The old meaning lives on. As a child I remember being bewildered that my mother would rub 'toilet water' all over her body after bathing.) Some anonymous marketing genius cleverly dreamed up the idea of associating the product with those benign activities of combing one's hair, putting on make-up or shaving. A woman would not be ashamed to go to her corner store (this is long before the anonymity of Walmart) and tell the smiling male clerk that she wanted to buy some 'toilet papers' to—um—use to curl her hair.

By 1880, the name and the product was in common use, as is evident from this article in *The New Hampshire Sentinel* of February 26th telling the story of Mr. George C. Fisk, a hometown boy made good:

> Mr. Fisk was born in Hinsdale owing to the good taste of his mother in selecting the charming location. When he had amassed the comfortable sum elsewhere, he came back to his native heath and built one of the prettiest and neatest paper mills in New England. The mills started up in 1873 and have run night and day ever since, turning out tons of manila paper. The operatives number thirteen – nine men and four girls. Last September they began the manufacture of toilet tissue paper, having Boston, New York and Springfield for their principal markets. They had just finished 400 cases for the Bay State Company when we visited the mills. The raw material is gunny sacks and manila rope from which they produce an average of twenty cases of toilet paper a day.

Only a small minority of the population, however, bought the manufactured item. Most people happily continued to use newspapers or catalogues, both of which had the supreme selling point of not costing anything. Only the most discriminating of tushes would pay the druggist for the packaged product. The thing that finally transformed toilet paper from a luxury item to a mass marketed necessity was the toilet itself. As we have seen, flush toilets began to come into general use starting in the late 1880s. Before the invention of this technological marvel, it didn't matter what you threw down the hole.

As you can see in this rare 1902 photograph looking down into the receptacle of a Lower East Side outhouse, one could toss all seventy-three pages of the Sunday edition of the New York Times into the pot and it wouldn't make much difference. Indeed, as urban archeologists have discovered digging through old cesspits, people tossed just about anything they didn't want into the stew from clay pipes and old socks to broken dishes.

The flush toilet with its ingenious 'S' trap was much fussier about what it ate. Too much paper or thick paper of the wrong sort would clog up the works, creating an unspeakable mess with the next flush.

As more and more people installed flush toilets in their homes, the thin tissue paper product first marketed by Mr. Gayetty became an absolute necessity for the peace of the household and its plumbing.

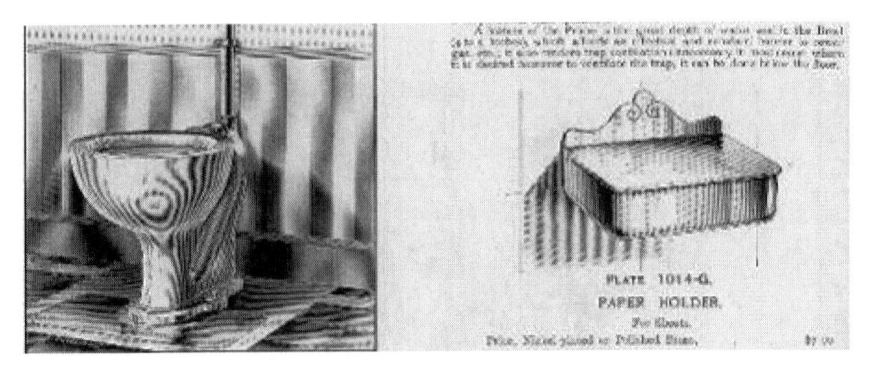

In this Mott Iron Works catalog entry for their 'Primo, Siphon Jet Water Closet', we see, included as an accessory, a wall-mounted paper holder—nickel plated, price, $7.00. The Deluge, pictured earlier also had two charmingly decorated porcelain paper holders built into the back of the seat.

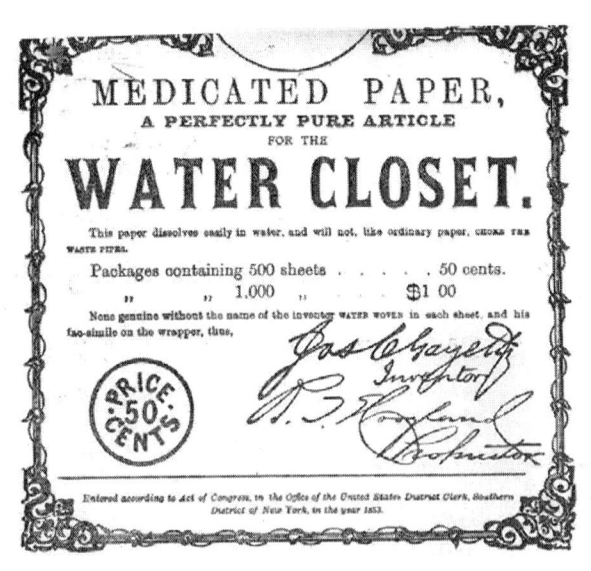

In later packaging, Gayetty dropped all references to piles. His only promise now: that his paper will dissolve so it "will not like ordinary paper choke the water pipes."

You can still buy toilet paper by the sheet like Gayetty's but only in two places. The first is at stores catering to orthodox Jews. Strictly religious Jews are forbidden by their religion from doing any work on the Sabbath. Tearing toilet paper from a roll is classified by certain rabbis as work, and therefore a product is available called "Shabbos Toilet

Paper." The package contains actual toilet paper precut into sheets and interleaved like facial tissue. A website selling this product warns that actual facial tissue "has sheets that are connected by tiny perforations" while their product promises no danger of tearing and therefore no danger of sinning.[54]

The second place you can buy toilet paper in sheets is in England where tradition reigns, and where it is employed in the highest offices of that land.

You will find no vulgar new-fangled rolls of toilet paper in Buckingham Palace. "By appointment to Her Majesty the Queen," Jeyes ensures that you and Liz can continue to wipe with toilet paper in flat sheets.

But in the 1880s, for the rest of the humanity, a new day was dawning in the realm of anal cleaning. In Albany, New York, we see the new vision slowly rising. And it was round.

6 ON A ROLL

When in 2011, the terrible tsunami stuck Japan, the citizens of Tokyo ran to their stores to grab the basic necessities of life. The stores' shelves were soon emptied of milk and canned goods. But the most highly prized item, first to disappear, was a product that did not even exist until the middle of the 19th century: rolls of toilet paper. In 2013, a toilet paper shortage in Venezuela almost brought down the government. For many people in the world, this humble consumer item has become a necessity of life.

Who was the Thomas Edison who created this commonplace product now present in several billion bathrooms around the world? Who invented toilet paper on a roll with those handy perforations? You would think that she or he would be as much a household name as the invention is a necessary part of every household.

The answer to this question is surprisingly difficult to unravel. Most reference books and Internet sites give the Scott Brothers of Philadelphia credit for inventing the toilet paper roll. The basis of this claim seems to come from Scott Paper Company literature, but I have found no sources from the 19th century in the form of patents or advertisements backing up this assertion. As we shall see, the Scott Brothers had an important role in the manufacturing and commercialization of toilet paper in the following century, but there is no evidence that they invented or were the first to market toilet paper on a roll. On the contrary, there is clear evidence that they were selling toilet paper in sheet form in the 1880s. They could not manufacture it in modern form because they did not hold the patents. That honor goes to someone else.

There are no statues erected to this man, nor will you find his biography in any *Who's Who in America*. We do not even have a picture of him. There is no lasting monument to him except the greatest one of all. About 2 billion people in the world touch his creation and his creation touches them at least once a day. His name: Seth Wheeler.

Seth Wheeler was born in upstate New York in 1838 and went to school in the state capital, Albany, where he studied mechanical engineering at the Albany Academy. On graduation he went to work at his father's company, Wheeler, Mechick & Co., which designed and manufactured farm equipment and became the largest concern of its kind in the eastern United States.

One of the big sellers was a Wheeler two-horse- power threshing machine. Real live horses trudging on a treadmill powered the patented device.

In this burgeoning world of small-scale manufacturing, Seth Wheeler became an entrepreneur and a capitalist in a 19th century America when those words actually meant something. He knew how to run a small company, and as an engineer he understood machines; he knew how to design them and build them. Above all, he was an inventor. His name is on more than 100 patents, including one in 1871 of vital interest to the present study.

As well as being farming country, upstate New York also was paper and lumber country. It had plentiful forests, waterfalls to power mills, and rivers to transport the products to large markets. We have seen how the demand for paper of all sorts was high, and it could be manufactured on an industrial scale. Putting to work his engineering knowledge of farm machinery, Wheeler entered the world of paper. His invention was one of those ideas that is so simple that it must have had other inventors around the country banging their heads that they didn't think of it themselves.

Seth Wheeler:
Improvement in Wrapping Paper.

117355   PATENTED JUL 25 1871

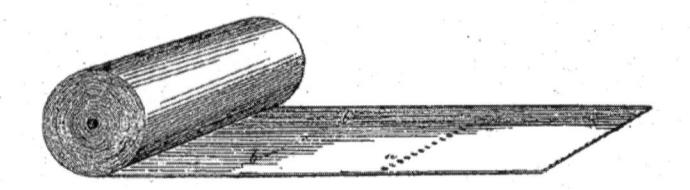

Although wrapping paper, like all paper is manufactured in rolls, prior to this invention, it had to be then cut into standard sized sheets by the manufacturer, counted out, bound up in bundles, and shipped to stores. As stated in his patent application, the existing process was expensive and time consuming; furthermore, the retailer would get bundles of paper with an unreliable count and whose edges often were damaged in transportation. Another problem with the older method: the cheap paper was made from wood pulp and, when exposed to air as individual sheets would, like week-old newspaper, become dry and brittle. The following is the quaint legalese of Wheeler's patent application:

> My invention is made for the purpose of avoiding or removing all the aforesaid difficulties or disadvantages; and consists in a roll of wrapping-paper with perforations on the line of the division between one sheet and the next, so as to be easily torn apart, such roll of wrapping paper forming a new article of manufacture.
>
> In preparing the roll of wrapping-paper the same is made in the usual machinery; but instead of being cut off in sheets the long belt of paper is perforated on the line of the division between one sheet and the next, so as to be easily torn at these lines, and then the paper is rolled into a compact roll.

$E = MC^2$ this ain't but it was a good and elegant idea that met a real need. Wheeler also had the mechanical know-how to build a machine that would perforate the rolls of paper. He set up a company to make and market his new product. Unfortunately it had a shaky start. The world was not quite ready for perforated rolls of wrapping paper. Undaunted, he reorganized and, in 1877, founded the Albany Perforated Wrapping Paper Company. This mouthful was abbreviated to the A.P.W. Paper Company because Seth's paper would soon begin to do a lot more than wrapping.

The sun did not stop in the sky when someone, somewhere, produced the planet's first roll of toilet paper. In truth, we probably will never know who did it or exactly when, but given the confluence of events—the introduction of flush toilets with their narrow drains, the existence of toilet paper in sheets since at least 1857 and the fact that paper is manufactured in rolls—the birth year of this new product was probably around 1877, the year A.P.W. was incorporated. Given his experience in producing paper products, prototype toilet paper roll number one may well have come from Seth Wheeler's plant. What is certain is that, with his patent and manufacturing experience, he held the key that would make the product a success.

England, at this time, had many more flush toilets than America did, and in 1880, a company run by Mr. Walter James Alcock which later became The British Patent Perforated Paper Company began importing and selling toilet paper manufactured by A.P.W. Three years later, licensing Wheeler's inventions, they began manufacturing it locally.[55] (You will read on many Internet sites the incorrect information that Mr. Alcock is the inventor of perforated toilet paper on a roll.)

In America, Wheeler had a few hurdles to overcome. First of all, he had the same problem that Gayetty had, convincing people to pay for toilet paper when so much free paper was available. Then, because his paper was coming in its totally new roll form, he also had to manufacture and convince customers to buy the fixture to dispense his product. His initial clients were hotels, the first places in the United States to install flush toilets on a large scale. Because toilets were new to most people, hotels had major problems with inexperienced flushers and clogged drains. Wheeler would sell hotels both the thin paper on a roll and the holder to dispense it. The hotel guests would be happy to use this wonderful product and, while wiping, would marvel at this wonder of the modern age. Hotel operators would be delighted as well because they would no longer have to contend with blocked toilets.

The 1880s were a period of extraordinary American entrepreneurial and inventive genius. Marvels such as the telephone, the phonograph, and the light bulb were invented in this country and either exported or franchised to many other countries. Wheeler and his creation were part of this wave of modernity. As well as in England, Wheeler set up subsidiaries in Canada, Germany, France, and Switzerland. Using his product, his patents and/or his equipment, toilet paper, in its familiar form, was beginning its conquest of the world.

In America, more and more individuals were installing flush toilets in their own homes, and these early adopters were also demanding the latest wiping technology. The 1880s were growing into toilet paper's perfect storm. Everything was in place: the need for this new product, the demand, and the manufacturing capacity. Other businessmen smelled huge profits and so there followed a perfect storm of patent applications. But Seth Wheeler continued to lead the pack:

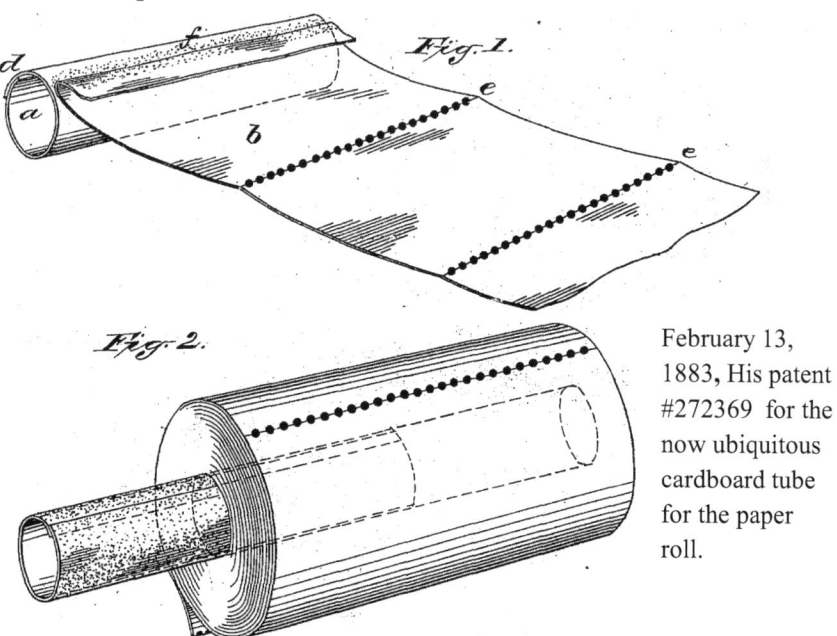

February 13, 1883, His patent #272369 for the now ubiquitous cardboard tube for the paper roll.

(No Model.) 2 Sheets—Sheet 1.

S. WHEELER.
TOILET AND WRAPPING PAPER HOLDER.

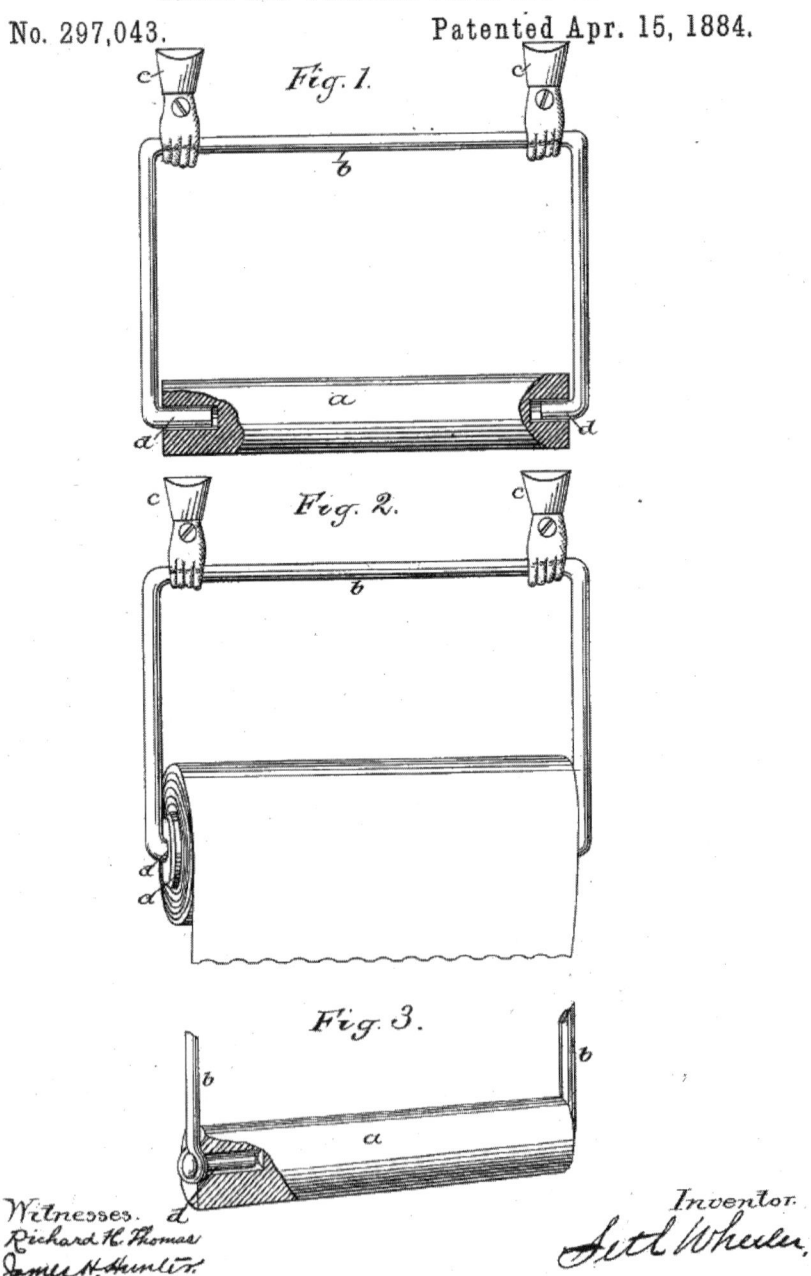

No. 297,043. Patented Apr. 15, 1884.

Fig. 1.

Fig. 2.

Fig. 3.

Witnesses.
Richard H. Thomas
James H. Hunter.

Inventor.
Seth Wheeler.

April 15, 1884, **Patent #297043**, Wheeler patents the toilet paper holder.

April 15, 1885 **Patent #297045**, he patents the mechanism inside the holder.

May 11, 1886 **Patent #341,709** he patents another style holder.

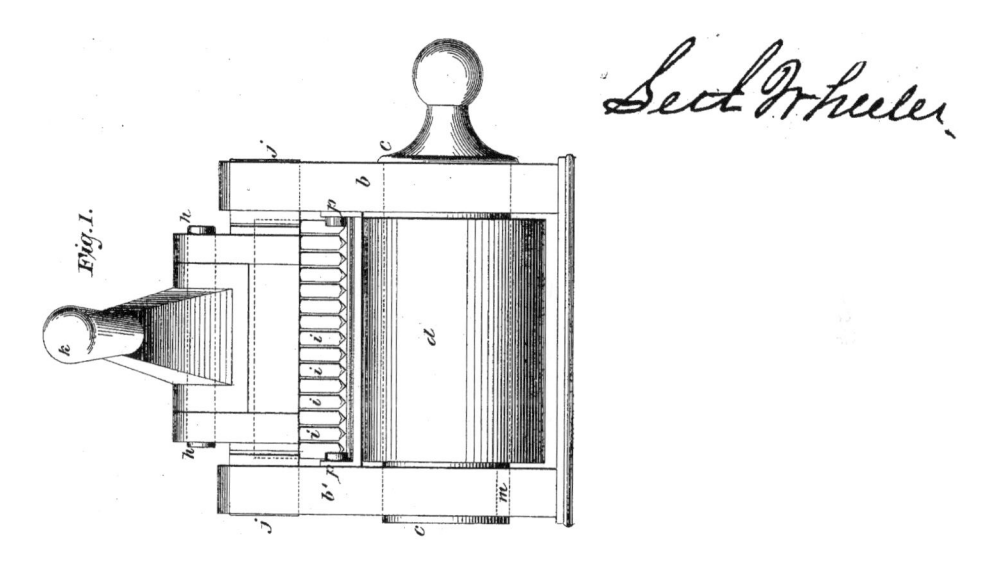

October 2, 1888 **Patent #390327**, Wheeler patents the machinery to perforate the toilet paper.

June 4, 1889. Patent **#404581**, Seth Wheeler patents a more advanced machine to perforate the paper.

February 4, 1890, Patent # **420,524**, Seth Wheeler patents paper cutting machinery.

March 4, 1890, **Patent # 422866**, He patents toilet paper perforated diagonally.

April 14, 1890, **Patent #438537,** He patents another style of toilet paper holder.

September 12, 1893, **Patent # 505767,** Seth Wheeler patents a device to impress ornamental patterns on the paper.

July 19, 1898, **Patent # 607498**, Wheeler patents toilet paper perforated to produce polygon sheets.

The preceding list gives only a few highlights of inventor Wheeler's creations. There are about 30 more, including many variations of the types of dispensers and the style of the rolls, but what has survived into the 21st century is the simple purity of his 1871 brainwave of putting perforations on a roll of paper.

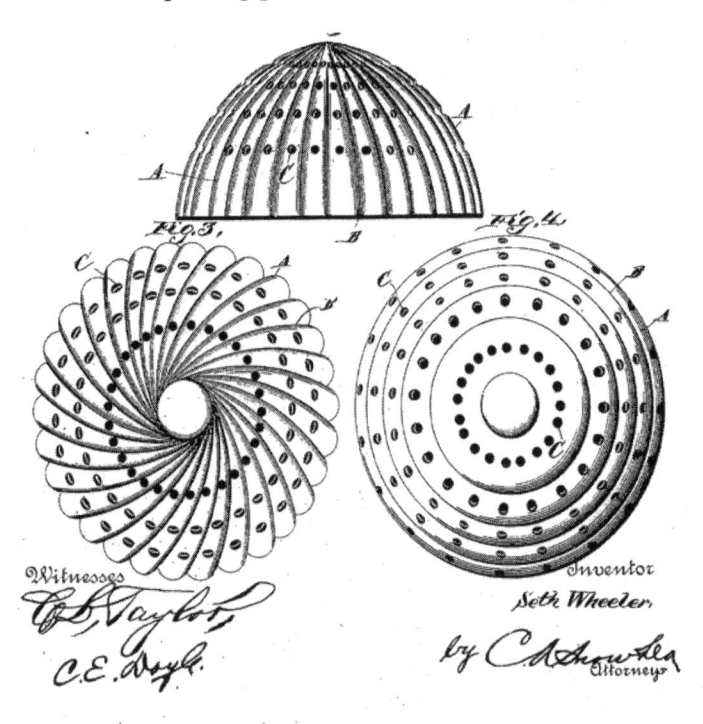

This Renaissance man turned out all kinds of different inventions almost at the rate that his machinery turned out toilet paper. Above is Wheeler's design for a bosom pad (whatever that is).

With his patents secured or pending, Wheeler could now introduce his new product to the general public. The advertisement on the next page is from the February 1884 issue of the prestigious Harper's Magazine.

Note that because of its new roll form, Wheeler offered potential buyers a package deal: 50 cents for a roll of paper and the fixture with the cute little hands that you could screw into the wall next to your newfangled toilet to dispense the roll. His pride of invention appears in the highly capitalized copy for this very early ad.

> Large expenditure for special machinery and in costly experiments, has enabled this Company to produce an article entirely free from any deleterious substance.
>
> Orders from ALL PARTS OF THE WORLD and endorsements, not only with respect to QUALITY but as regards ECONOMY, CONVENIENCE and NEATNESS warrant the claim of superiority.
>
> There is entire freedom from litter and waste and the DIVISION INTO SHEETS BY PERFORATIONS SECURES AN ECONOMY in use UNATTAINABLE in the UNPERFORATED Roll first made by us

He was not exaggerating his invention's worldwide fame. Wheeler's British agents were marketing his creation not only to England but to their colonies around the world. In a London newspaper from 1885, we see The British Patent Perforated Paper Company advertisement using Wheeler's trademarked cute little hands holding the 'revolving roller':

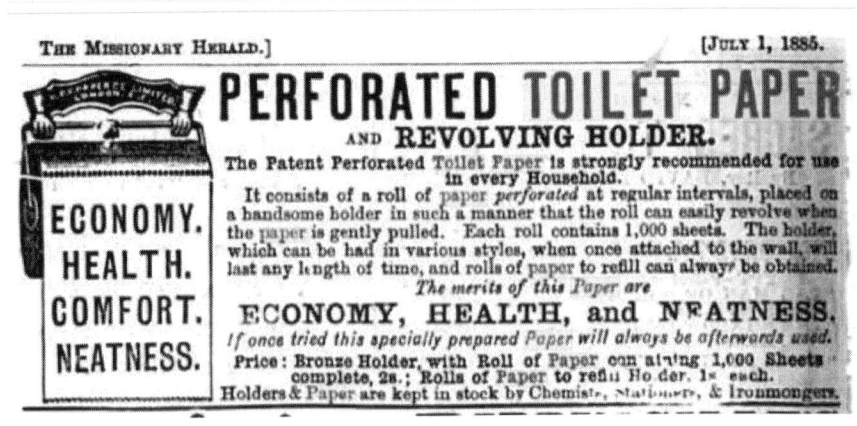

Wheeler was patenting every possible permutation of paper and machinery in the 1880s and 1890s because he knew that he was not alone in the field. Others saw this disposable consumer product as a gold mine and there followed a flurry of other patents from the most basic to the most bizarre. In the latter category we find patent number 1,139,351 by a Mr. Danner.

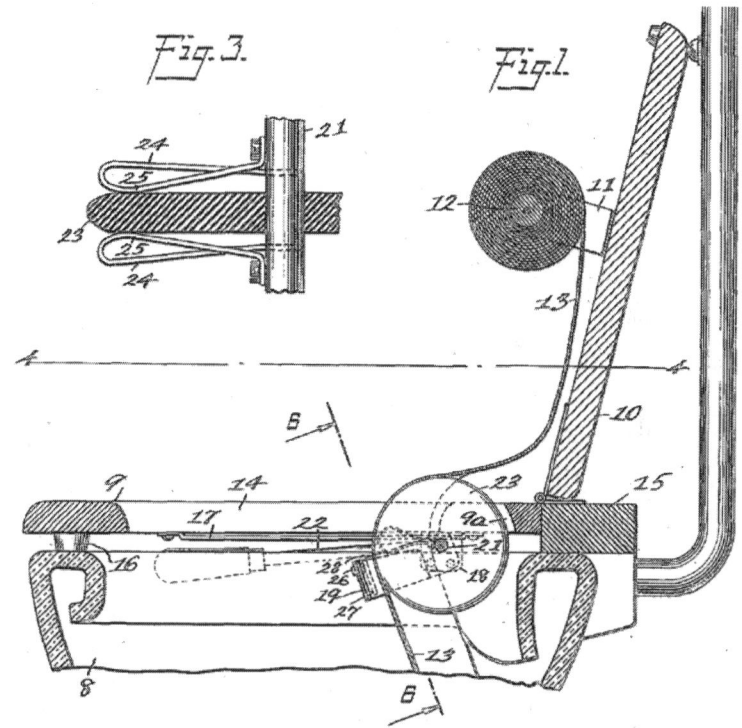

This device of mind-boggling complexity allows the defecator to pull handle #22 and the roll of paper would wipe his or her ass. All this with the subject not having to touch his or her anal area while still sitting on the toilet. This gadget, had it ever been built, would have been a mechanical version of The Groom of the King's Close-Stool. With it, everyone could be like Henry VIII.

Many inventors tried to address the problem of the toilet paper glutton—the individual who seems to need half a roll of paper to do the wiping, breaking the household budget as well as the household plumbing. The simplest and most elegant solution was the brainwave of Mr. Oliver Hewlett Hicks. This, in almost biblical language, is his patent application:

Heretofore toilet-paper has usually been furnished to the public either in the form of sheets cut to the proper size for use or in cylindrical rolls of continuous lengths. In some cases the paper furnished in the form of rolls has been perforated transversely at regular intervals, with the view of enabling the user to separate it into sheets of uniform size, and thus obtain the advantages of the package composed of independent sheets. The chief objection to each of these modes of furnishing toilet-paper is the great amount of wastage which occurs. Where the separate-sheet plan is employed the user is apt to detach a great many more sheets than he actually uses, while where the roll plan is practiced the rolls are usually hung so as to freely revolve, and the user, by a pull upon the depending end, oftentimes recklessly reels off yards where feet would answer.

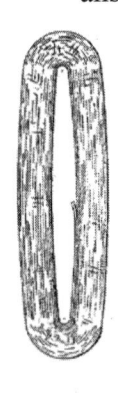

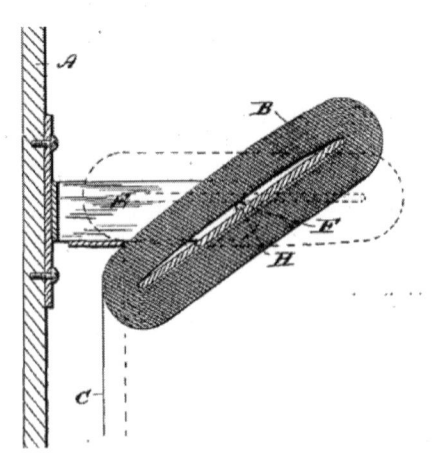

Mr. Hicks's ingenious solution to toilet paper recklessness was to supply it, not with a round core, but an oblong core for which he designed this dispenser, patent #325,174. The dispenser turns only half a rotation with each pull and then breaks at the perforation so the reckless offender gets only one sheet per pull.

Every major invention of the 19th and 20th century was accompanied by hard-fought patent cases making the lawyers rich and the inventors poor. You would think that such a cash cow as toilet paper, whose invention was covered by hundreds of competing patents, would have engendered similar fights. In fact, there was only one big one. A large concern called, oddly enough, The Morgan Envelope Company, bought Hicks's invention and began marketing a toilet paper called 'The Oval King' with its own special Oval King dispenser. (You can still find them on Ebay.)

Wheeler knew a good thing when he saw it and jumped on the oval bandwagon stealing the idea and patenting the device himself in England (a fact that a judge would later call reprehensible but not illegal). But when he started to manufacture A.P.W. paper in oval form to be used in Morgan's dispenser, Morgan cried foul and sued. In 1894 the case went all the way up to the U.S. Supreme Court with: MORGAN ENVELOPE CO v. ALBANY PERFORATED WRAPPING PAPER CO., 152 U.S. 425 (1894)[56]. In this complex case, one of the issues discussed was this: if you make and patent a device, can someone else supply the item that this device uses? The courts ultimately ruled against Morgan and for our hero Wheeler. It turned out to be a landmark decision establishing a principle that covers every product manufactured for something else from needles for sewing machines or phonographs to cassettes for audio recorders to USB flash drives for computers. The case is cited and its merits continue to be argued in hundreds of university law review articles. This is just another example of the ways that this simple product has changed the world.

When not inventing, Wheeler was president of the Wheeler Heat and Power Company; vice-president of the Cheney Piano Action Company of Castleton, NY and a director of both the Albany County Savings Bank and the New York State Bank. You wonder how he had time to eat. Wheeler died in 1925 but you will not find an obituary of this great American in any major newspaper.

Albany Perforated continued making toilet paper into the 1930s, but it was another creative and marketing genius who carried forth the toilet paper torch. This individual transformed his company from a mom and pop operation into an industrial and consumer superpower.

> I've learned that life is like a roll of toilet paper.
> The closer it gets to the end, the faster it goes.
>
> Andy Rooney

The 135 year rise and fall and the resurrection of The Scott Paper Company is one of the epic stories in the history of American enterprise. The saga of this mighty empire built on a foundation of toilet paper is taught in business schools as an object lesson of both successful and failed management. The Albany Perforated Wrapping Paper Company was the coming attraction. Scott would become the blockbuster.

The beginnings of what would become the largest most successful company in the 150 year history of toilet paper were modest indeed. The Company was formed as a limited partnership in 1874 by two bewhiskered Yankee gentlemen, Clarence and Irvin Scott, and their cousins. Their total capital, $4,536.40. Their business was toilet paper and their operation was bare-bones. Irvin and Clarence Scott would buy suitable paper in bulk from various suppliers and then cut it into sheets, re-package it, and sell it to retailers.

Quakers and staunch Republicans, in an era when the Republican Party was the progressive party, the brothers soon assumed leadership of the company. Scrupulously honest, they had the aura of Sunday school teachers. Clarence, tall and dignified, always wore a stiff white shirt and high-standing collar even in the sweltering Philadelphia summer. He had another quality vital to the company's success; he was a fabulous salesman.

Their business plan was simple and ingenious. Remember that in the Victorian era the product they were marketing was an unmentionable distributed either by mail order or secreted under the counter in pharmacies along with other unmentionables. It would only be offered to those embarrassed customers who dared ask for it as a 'medical item.' Scott's strategy was to give the store owners a proprietary interest in pushing the product by customizing the size and form of the package to their specifications. Most important, the Scotts would put the store's name on the wrapper. Along with baby powder and cold cream you would be sold 'Smith Pharmacy Toilet Tissue' with the Smith logo on the package from trusted Mr. Smith himself, who naturally would take pride in 'his' brand.

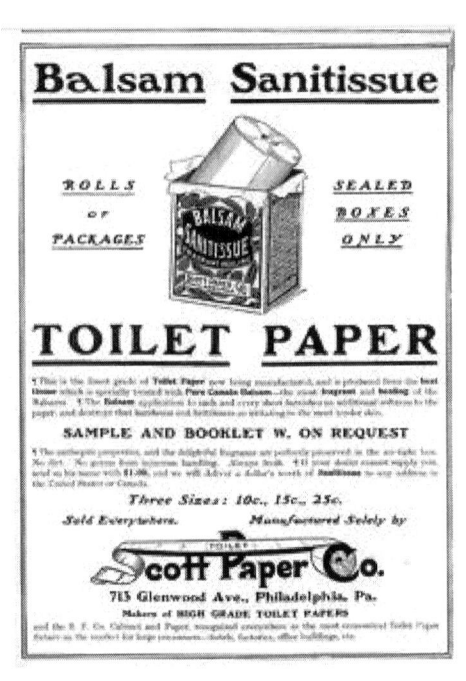

Some books and Internet sites will tell you that Clarence and Irvin used different brand names because they were ashamed to have their family name on such a product. Not true: as we see in this ad, they were proud of having their name associated with the product and even used Irvin's wife's maiden name, Hoyt, as one of the brands. One fact nobody questions: with this private label arrangement, they were making a lot of money.

Their timing could not have been better. As we have seen, with the introduction of flush toilets in American cities, this former so-called medical item was well on the way to becoming a household necessity. With their product more and more in demand, the Scott Brothers prospered. In 1899 the company was incorporated with a capital of $100,000 and they built a four-story building in Philadelphia, then the largest structure in the world devoted to the manufacture of toilet paper.[57] The Scotts were supplying paper to over 2000 retailers under hundreds of different brand names. Their customers included variety stores, department stores, and a new kind of self-service store which had just been opened in Lancaster, Pennsylvania by a Mr. F. W. Woolworth. Clearly, in 25 years, what had started out as a modest operation was poised to become a very big business—little did they dream how big.

Enter Arthur Scott.

Arthur Scott was Irvin's only son. On graduation from posh Swarthmore College, the last thing he wanted to do was to spend his life selling toilet paper. But at age 21 this dutiful son agreed to enter the family business. Around the turn of the century, with the company booming, he made a radical suggestion: Scott Paper was now ready to market its own brand of toilet paper. The woodchips must have really flown at company headquarters on Glenwood Avenue when the young Scott broached the subject to his father and uncle. These 19th century self-made men had created a business from scratch and were not about to change their ways. Arthur persisted, knowing that branding was the way of the future. In 1902, the founders relented giving him permission to test his new-fangled theory. Arthur bought the trademark rights to a brand they were already producing with the classy name, 'Waldorf'.

At the turn of the last century, the idea of branding—advertising and packaging a standardized product or service—was an innovative business model. It was showing promise in marketing everything from soap to restaurants. But would it work with toilet paper? After a shaky beginning, Arthur's idea took off. Scott's yearly sales soon topped $500,000. By then the company had completely ceased making private-label brands and was selling only Scott-branded toilet paper. And Arthur was rapidly proving himself the Steve Jobs of the sanitary paper industry by next inventing a completely new product that Americans didn't even know they needed. One day a carload of paper was delivered to the factory that was too thick to be manufactured into toilet paper. Thinking on his feet, Arthur had it cut into wider rolls and perforated and sold as disposable paper towels. This child of toilet paper was a huge success and the trees of the world have never been safe since that time.

In 1911, Arthur Scott took another enormous risk. Up to this point, Scott was buying paper from other mills and simply cutting it and packaging it. Now, with his own brands to support, he needed to control the quality of the paper itself. This meant setting up a plant to manufacture the paper from scratch—an enormous investment in equipment and personnel. Using the company's little capital as collateral, he borrowed money to buy three buildings and a power plant in the town of Chester, Pennsylvania, as well as two cylinder-type paper making machines each capable of spewing out 76-inch master rolls of toilet paper at a speed of 200 feet a minute.

During the teens, Arthur Scott and his engineers poured huge sums of money into research and development. The process of making the soft toilet paper that we know today is called 'creping' and it occurs during the drying cycle of the paper-manufacturing process. At this point, with the sheet stuck to the huge steel cylinder in the machinery, it is scraped (or creped) off by a metal blade. The resulting paper is weak and of low density but absorbent and flexible. Unlike the toilet paper of the 19th century which, at best, had the feel of tissue paper, Scott was producing not only the greatest quantity of toilet paper in the world, but also paper of exceptional quality for its intended use. Chester, PA, had become the toilet paper capital of the world.

Arthur Hoyt Scott became President of the company in 1921 and pushed Scott Paper to heights undreamed of by its founders. Ultimately his empire built on toilet paper owned forests of trees in the United States and Canada, pulp and paper mills in 21 countries; it had 30,000 employees and sales of over five billion dollars. Sadly, he did not to live to see the culmination of his vision. He died of a stroke, at the age 52 in 1927, two years after that other toilet paper pioneer, Seth Wheeler. Unlike Wheeler, this now powerful industrialist was honored in *Who's Who* and received a half-column obituary in *The New York Times*. This sweet-smelling headline, however, says it all:

Arthur Hoyt Scott dies:
Founder of The American Peony Society

The article mentions in passing that he was a paper manufacturer but extols at length all his horticultural activities. The obituary details the plantings in the impressive garden of his country estate and lists all the clubs he belonged to and included the fact that, in addition to his peony activities, he was also treasurer of the American Iris Society. In all of these two hundred sweet- smelling words, the 'newspaper of record' carefully avoids mentioning the fact that Arthur Hoyt Scott perfected and popularized one of the most useful and ubiquitous consumer products in the world.

Writers in the Scott Company internal newspaper mourned the loss of the much admired 'Mr. Arthur' and eulogized his memory with a poem by R. L. Sharpe:

> *Isn't it strange that princes and kings,*
> *And clowns that caper in sawdust rings,*
> *And common folks like you and me*
> *Are builders for eternity?*

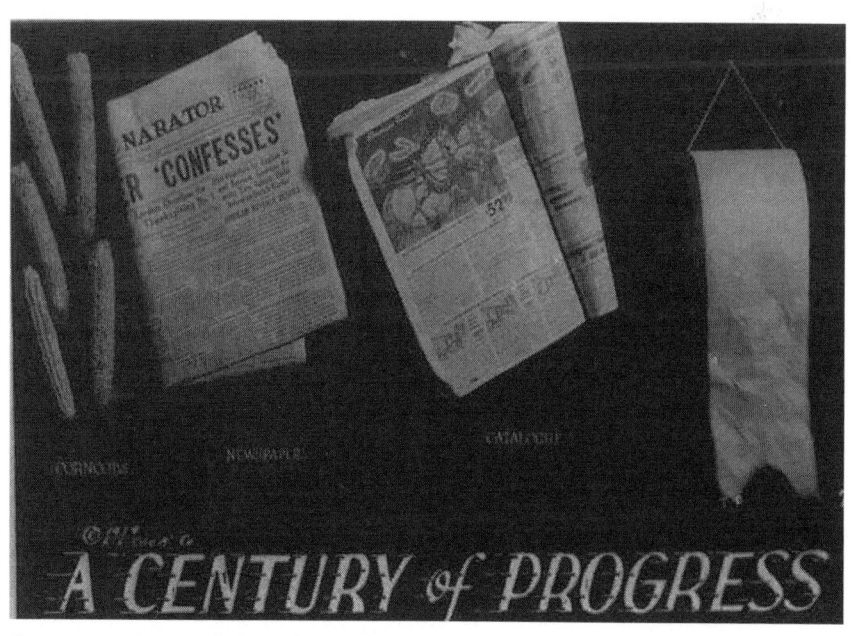

A postcard parodying the motto of the 1933 Chicago World's Fair.

Board of Directors

We began the tale of Scott Paper by describing it as a dramatic rise, fall, and resurrection. We now come to the fall and resurrection part of this story. This formidable group of men—and they were all men—ran the company in the early 1950s and took what was already an extremely profitable concern into the financial stratosphere.

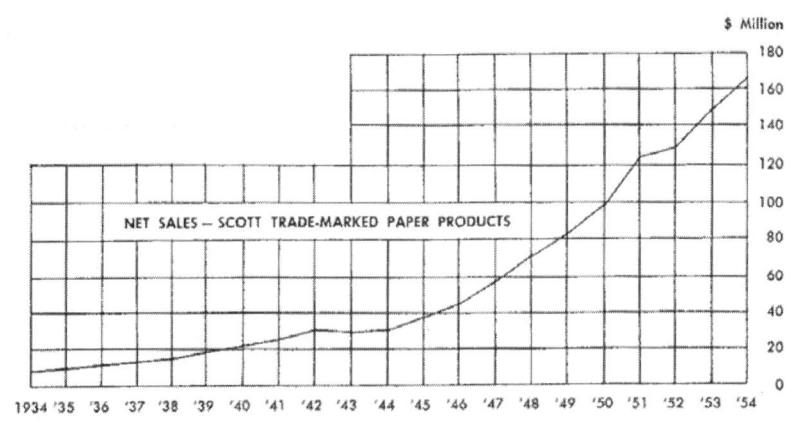

Year after year the graphs showing sales and profits of Scott paper products went straight up, from under one hundred million in 1950 to $700 million by the end of the 1960s. In his annual report in 1953, President of the Board, Thomas B. MaCabe (center left)

warned that "we must guard against giving any impression of wanting to grab too big a piece of the pie."[58] Their biggest problem, it seems, was to be seen as being <u>too</u> successful because, in terms of making and selling toilet paper and similar sanitary paper products, they held a near monopoly.

But as I sat in the library leafing through year after year of the Scott's Annual Report to its shareholders, each one more glossy than next, I began to get an uneasy feeling. The booklets were presented with elaborately staged photos of beautiful fashion models, computers, almost everything but what continued to be the core source of the company's enormous profits. In the 1960s the reports document a major push for diversification. First came an enormous investment in plants to produce so-called coated paper—a product used to print glossy magazines and catalogs. Granted that Scott was still in the paper business, but the equipment and expertise to manufacture that type of paper was completely different from the activity they had become so good at, producing so-called sanitary paper. But then they reported diversification farther afield. Scott was now manufacturing underpads for carpets, foam insulating materials for buildings, lighting fixtures, and finally lawn furniture. Lawn Furniture! It was obvious to even a casual observer like myself that something was going terribly wrong in the upper regions of Scott management. Admittedly toilet paper isn't glamorous, but were they ashamed of how they made money? Or were they just following the capitalist imperative that you must constantly grow and expand or the company will die?

Whatever the cause of these forays into new industries and products, the results were disastrous. For the first time in the 100 year history of the company, the profit graphs began to level off and then decline—from a 1988 income of over 400 million dollars, to a 1990 income of under 150 million dollars to a 1991 company *loss* of 70 million dollars. Its corporate bonds, once the most solid in American industry, were downgraded to just above junk. "I guess...we took on too many projects at once," said CEO Philip Lippincott. [59] Bleeding money, the company started downsizing, laying off 3000 workers, including Chairman Lippincott. In 1994, the board announced the appointment of a new CEO—'chainsaw' Albert Dunlop, a so-call turnaround specialist known for his slash and burn tactics. Dunlop slashed and burned most of the company's employees and its executives and reduced Scott paper to its "core competencies"— manufacturing and selling toilet paper and related products. With the company much smaller but profitable again, it was gobbled up by its former archrival, Kimberly-Clark of Kleenex fame. Under their vast corporate wing, the Scott brand continues to be sold to this day and the Chester plant built by horticulturalist 'Mr. Arthur' continues to roll on at the rate of over two million rolls a day.

So, in the end, this epic tale has come full circle. Born in the humble beginnings of toilet paper in the 1870s, Scott lives on into its third century, having returned to its core value—toilet paper.

SELLING IT

The 1920s were the golden age of American advertising. They had to be. Before this time, the major problem of industry was production—how to turn out enough cars, cans and consumables to meet the demand. Now with assembly lines and mechanization, factories were turning out more stuff than they could sell, and so manufacturers had to create an artificial demand for their products. Fortunately they had new and powerful weapons. High-speed printing ensured that everyone would have access to newspapers and colorful magazines; then there was that miracle of the air—radio—which brought the soothing voice of the salesmen into almost every American home. Finally there was a new science of advertising employing psychologists and statisticians to fine-tune and make irresistible the message to buy. Americans could now spend money they didn't have using that other wonderful creation—credit. And spend they did, buying toasters, washing machines, cars, radios, and new homes—all on credit.

Marketing and advertising toilet paper, however, posed huge problems for any company trying to sell it. *To this day* you can only hint at what the product actually does. But the earlier marketers had an even bigger problem; its name. By the early 20th century, the word 'toilet' had worn out its euphemistic welcome—a toilet was a toilet, the thing you shit in, so the name 'toilet paper' was now forbidden. Scott solved the problem by called the stuff 'bathroom tissue,' in one swoop eliminating the offensive word 'toilet' and even the now questionable word 'paper'. When the euphemism 'bathroom' had become too evocative they dropped even that. "Don't ask for toilet paper," this ad from 1919 explains; the lady of the house can just ask the store clerk for ScotTissue.

Avoid Embarrassment

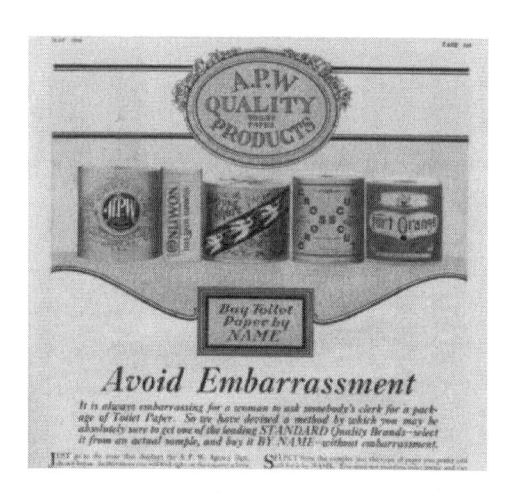

The Albany Perforated Wrapping Paper Company used its convoluted name to do one better on Scott. "Avoid Embarrassment", the headline in this ad from 1920 says. And then goes into detail. "It is always embarrassing for a woman to ask somebody's clerk for a package of Toilet Paper. So we've devised a method..." Ask for A.P.W.

In a tube—seven rolls of this remarkable bathroom paper, a sanitary and convenient package, now delivered to your home for one dollar. It saves both embarrassment and money to simply ask for a tube of "Northern Tissue."

The winner in this peculiar dance of avoidance must go to the Northern Tissue ad from 1921. Now, not only can a woman avoid using the dreaded words 'toilet paper' but she can completely escape the humiliation of talking to 'someone's clerk'. Northern will wingedly deliver their 'bathroom paper' directly to your home in such a large quantity that you will only have to confront a smirking mailman once every few months.

If car and toaster manufacturers had an overproduction problem, Scott Paper had it in spades. They had the capacity to roll out much more toilet paper than they could retail. The pressure was to do some explicit selling, but advertising something that you can't name or talk about presented major creative problems. (As late as the 1970s, for example, the Standards and Practices Department of the American Broadcasting Company still would not allow advertisers to use the words 'toilet paper'.[60])

Fortunately these were the 1920s when the times really were a-changing. Short skirts, flappers, illicit alcohol, the movies, and a recognition of the insanity of World War One had dissolved the Puritanical mores of the Victorian era. Kimberly-Clark was attempting to promote their new invention, Kotex disposable menstrual pads. In 1923, with some very clever copywriting —part of the wardrobe of daintiness—they broke the taboo and began a major, highly successful campaign of advertising in magazines and newspapers.

"Don't sell the steak," advertisers tell their clients, "sell the sizzle." During the 1920s Scott developed a subtle advertising campaign linking their unmentionable product with elegance, modernity, and sophistication:

Women sense it immediately

—that atmosphere of elegance and refinement—those necessary little appointments, noticed but not discussed, which contribute so much to the comfort and well-being of guests and family.

ScotTissue has made a place for itself in well-conducted homes. It is the choice of discriminating women everywhere, because of its hygienic purity and safety.

A highly-absorbent, snow-white, soothing tissue, marvelously soft as fine old linen. Kind to the most sensitive skin. Peculiarly adapted to the needs of women of intuitive daintiness. Ask your doctor.

No conversation. Just say "ScotTissue" to your storekeeper and receive a big, economical, dustproof roll.

SCOTT PAPER COMPANY, Chester, Pa.

15 cents a roll

"Women of intuitive daintiness" in the height of 1920s fashion shown here at tea would only buy the best of those "necessary little appointments, noticed but not discussed." The message: 'by thy toilet paper we shall know thee'. It may be a new era, but in a world before supermarkets where you still have to confront a smirking sales clerk: To save this humiliation, "No conversation, Just say ScotTissue to your storekeeper."

In 1927, with the death of 'Mr. Arthur', Scott Paper had evolved from a family business into a modern corporation. Scott Paper had the most advanced production facilities in the world. Their engineers had designed and built three $750,000 machines, (add two zeros to convert to today's dollars), each the size of half a football field, that could each spew out toilet paper at 1000 feet a minute. In that year alone, they were selling about 40 million rolls of toilet paper to American's one hundred and twenty million rear ends. If they could sell more, they could easily manufacture it.

Scott's new management decided that a radical change in their marketing was needed. They hired the legendary J. Walter Thomson advertising agency. JWT's advertising had made every brand from Ford to Kellogg into household names around the world and, at the same time, made these companies' stockholders extremely wealthy. The firm's president, Stanley Resor, was a giant in the advertising world. Resor claimed to have turned the art of advertising into a science. His company's psychologists worked tirelessly to exploit the deep unconscious drives that motivate all human beings—love, fear, and hate. In the fear department, advertisers invented a way of talking about the unmentionables. You couldn't use the words 'bad breath' in advertising so copywriters invented the medical-sounding word, 'halitosis.' Because of halitosis you could lose friends, lovers, and your job. Listerine would bring sweetness to your breath and a return of success and happiness. You couldn't mention body odor so some genius came up with the term 'B.O.' and, as we have seen, deodorants also promised to bring your friends and lovers near to your body again. Using Lysol as a douche for 'intimate feminine hygiene' promised to rejuvenate your marital sex life. Sometimes the claims required an even greater stretch of credulity. The laxative Jujol was said by JWT copywriters to promote "a clear, radiant, youthful complexion." All of the agency's creative talent was now focused on selling more and more ScotTissue. In the increasingly competitive world of toilet paper, the gloves were off, or as in the case of the following ad, the gloves were horrifyingly on.

Toilet Tissue Illness..

is unpleasant to think about!

Through a microscope the edge of inferior toilet tissue reveals a roughness and irregularity. Such tissues, doctors say, cause serious injury to delicate membranes.

A PROMINENT intestinal specialist lists fifteen forms of rectal disease which may be directly caused or aggravated by inferior bathroom tissue.

Yet, unless they are extremely careful to demand a high-grade tissue, housewives may be sold paper which is totally unfit for bathroom use.

Many so-called toilet tissues sold today are not toilet tissue at all, but only ordinary tissue paper cut in rolls.

They may be glazed to a hard finish—non-absorbent, actually injurious to delicate membranes.

Some are chemically harmful—made from reclaimed waste materials.

ScotTissue, Sani-Tissue and Waldorf are three famous tissues which meet all the requirements medical authorities say toilet tissue must have to be safe: *softness, absorbency, chemical purity.*

They are extremely absorbent—without being blotter-like. And absorbency,
as all doctors say, is absolutely essential to proper cleansing.

Scott Tissues are prepared from the finest, fresh materials . . . specially processed to cleanse the most sensitive skin—harmlessly, comfortably. They are unusually soft and actually cloth-like.

Crumple a sheet. Feel the *suave texture,* the absence of harsh fibres. Even your hand can often detect the sharp edges of ordinary glazed tissue.

Take no chances with the tissue you buy for your bathrooms. Always ask for Scot-Tissue, Sani-Tissue, Waldorf.

SCOTTISSUE
2 *for* 25¢
Prices for U.S. only

Scott Tissues
"Soft as Old Linen"

Dealers are also offering Sani-Tissue, the new popular priced white toilet tissue with the same health-protecting qualities

October 1930 Good Housekeeping

No longer would you just seem to be inelegant to your friends: 'buy the wrong brand,' Mrs. Housewife, 'and you could be causing you and your family great harm, or even worse!' Scott hired PR people to re-enforce the idea that other brands of toilet paper could not only cause hemorrhoids but even rectal cancer.

Despite their enormous manufacturing capacity and a superior soft paper, Scott, in the late 1920s, had captured only a small percentage of the potential market. They were competing against not only other large companies like Northern Tissue, but also hundreds of other companies who were buying paper in bulk from the mills and repackaging it under their own brand names. This toilet paper was often less expensive than Scott Tissue and much less expensive than Scott's 'luxury' brand 'Waldorf'. These competing brands were not standardized and of variable quality. Scott's largest competitor, however, remained the free stuff. Most Americans, including the more than 50% who did not have access to flush toilets, were still using newspaper, Sears catalog pages, and corn cobs for economical and effective wiping. Many sensible housewives, particularly during the Depression, decided that if they were to save money on anything, their first line of economy would be the stuff that was used once and thrown down the hole. The USP (unique selling proposition) of Scott was that their toilet paper, unlike that of many of their competitors and the free stuff, was soft and free from chemicals. By creating this fantastical rectal panic they gave housewives—in advertising lingo—a 'reason why' that they would never dare to ignore:

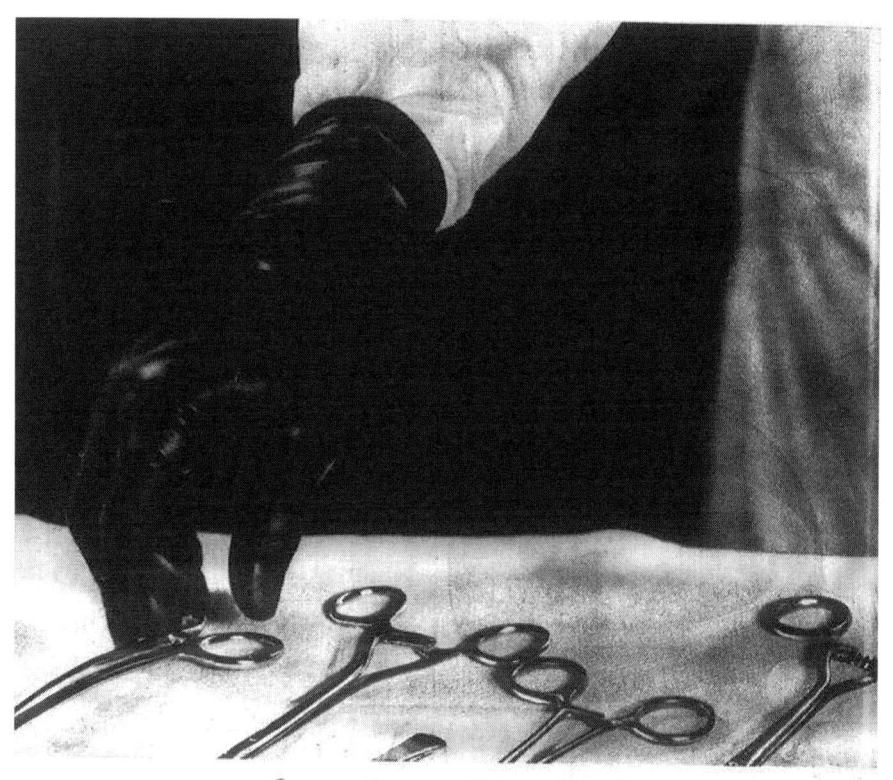

... often the only relief from toilet tissue illness

Northern Tissue joined in the scare-fest with an ad from 1935. In the ad they implied that the inferior toilet paper of their competitors is imbedded with tiny splinters of wood. "Remember", the copy intoned, "toilet tissue touches the most delicate membranes of the body" and "there are no splinters in Northern Tissue."

And if the woman of the house still insisted on buying "rough" toilet paper, the following advertisement from 1939, in the form of a comic strip, predicted something much worse than hemorrhoids.

From the late 1920s into the 1940s, Scott paper pounded out many variations on the theme but all had the same message—fear. In the 1930s, Scott became one of this country's largest advertisers in newspapers, magazines and the new medium of radio. During the Depression, while other companies were failing left and right, Scott spent over one million dollars to expand their facilities. In Chester, Pennsylvania, their huge Fourdrinier paper machines were now being run 24 hours a day in four shifts to keep up the demand they had created. By 1940, Scott had become the largest maker of toilet paper in the world. Such is the genius of advertising.

And speaking of 'rough' toilet paper, back in merry old England, the British Patent Perforated Paper company kept turning out rolls of aptly named *Bronco*, the hard and shiny toilet paper developed in the 1880s (and the bane of the delicate tushes of American tourists). It continued to be marketed into the late 1980s with nothing more to offer than Wheeler's perforations and memories of Imperial glory.

Before the British Motor Car
even before the opening of Tower Bridge
The British Patent Perforated Paper Company were leading Manufacturers of Toilet Paper

Looking at toilet paper ads today both in the United States and around the world, we find lots of babies, rabbits, puppies, pussy cats, and clouds. We have come a long way from Scott's ominous surgical knives. But search hard as we might, we still fail to find an ad that dares to directly extol what the product actually does: that it wipes excrement from your rectum.

In the rude, rough country of Australia, however, lacking the Puritan traditional squeamishness about all things bodily and a continuing pioneering ethos, we come closest to associating a popular brand, 'Quilton' toilet paper, with what it actually does. We still have the clouds and the baby but all the ads end with the slogan ringing in the consumers' ears: "Quilton loves your bum"

The arrow in the butt and the cut line were the brainchild of Henry Ngai, president of ABC Tissue, and this campaign resulted in his brand 'Quilton' capturing 30% of the large Australian toilet paper market. [61]

When they cannot think of anything else, the advertiser can always fall back on sex, as in these truly weird ads for Renova toilet paper from Spain.

Toilet paper has been advertised and aggressively marketed for over a century. Billions of dollars, tons of newsprint, and hours of radio and television time has been expended on selling us, first on the idea of using toilet paper, and then convincing us to purchase a particular brand. Every imaginable device in the advertiser's lexicon has been employed to this end. But in spite of all their efforts, a huge untapped market still exists. The fact that the toilet paper marketers must face is this: two thirds of the world's 6 billion people find the *very idea* of cleaning their rears with a dry piece of paper—no matter how soft, colorful or absorbent—completely repulsive!

WATER

Different cultures, different wipes

In matters of how to clean one's rear, the world is divided into two camps, the wipers and the washers. With religious fervor, each side is convinced that they are cleaning their asses the only way possible and the others are disgusting, unhygienic, or even blasphemous. This split is not even. The world has more wipers than washers, and probably most people reading these pages are in this former school. For that reason, I intend to make the strong case for the washers. For wipers, the idea of directly handling one's own shit, even using the medium of water, is seen as filthy and nauseating. It is not even clear to wipers how washers actually do it. The scientific and medical evidence, however, all supports one side of this argument and is indisputable—the washers have cleaner butts.

Every few years Dr. Phillip Tierno, director of the Department of Microbiology and Pathology at the NYU School of Medicine, terrifies germ-phobic New Yorkers by swabbing everything from door knobs to subway poles in search of fecal organisms deposited by the hands of the city's eight million unwashed or poorly washed citizens. After reading the results of his swabbing you would never want to touch a drinking fountain, an elevator button, or a handrail again. Reporters from *The New York Post* swabbed the door handle of their rival newspaper, *The Daily News* and gleefully reported that the bacterial count was off the charts. Shit residue was also found on $20 bills from ATM machines, on the hand grips of exercise machines at a gym, on the menus of fancy restaurants, on the door handles of the City's Department of Health building and those of such high-class establishments as Tiffany's and the Plaza Hotel. Also crawling with such fecal, diarrhea-inducing organisms as e.coli and staphylococcus are the seats of the Upper East Side subway cars, limousines, and the center orchestra seats of Broadway theaters. Clearly, even high-class American butts have a lot of explaining to do.

The cause is easily explained—toilet paper. The use of toilet paper alone leaves a lot of shit behind on the behind, and the microscopic bugs can easily pour out through one's pants or skirts and deposit themselves to any waiting chair. And, what may be surprising to some, the use of toilet paper leaves excrement on one's hands. Dr. R. I. Hutchinson discovered this fact while investigating the causes of dysentery spread by fecal contamination:

> The permeability of toilet paper was investigated by wrapping a double thickness of the paper over the fingers, which were then pressed lightly on to solid, semisolid, and fluid stools for a few seconds. Five different types of paper were used, including two proprietary disinfectant brands, and in every case, organisms penetrated through to the fingers with the fluid and semisolid stools. With the solid stools, 80% of the papers allowed the passage of organisms through to the fingers. Experimental [analysis] in the laboratory showed that the organisms remained alive on the fingers for about three hours. [62]

To the average microbes, toilet paper acts like a sieve; they easily pass through it onto our hands. This fact is proved by a suggestion for a nifty classroom experiment for high school biology teachers proposed by Christopher Woolverton of Kent State University. He details a procedure to determine exactly how many layers will actually block the transmission of infectious agents. His results:

three layers, with little difference among brands, or whether it is single or two ply paper.[63]

Since most of us do not use three layers of toilet paper and since many of us do not wash our hands with soap and hot water after defecation, almost 1/3 of the population has "bacteria of faecal origin on their hands."[64] The Muslim washers of the world, whom we find so disgusting because they use their fingers to pick out every trace of excrement from their behinds, are more likely by the nature of the anal cleaning operation and their religion to wash their hands thoroughly after defecation. So with whom would you rather shake hands? Where would you rather sit now? What is more disgusting?

And then there is the issue of how clean is one's butt. Practitioners of the water school insist that the smearing of our rears with toilet paper, no matter how thick and soft, just doesn't do the job. As one shocked Bangladeshi, on finding out that Westerners used toilet paper exclaimed to a British doctor, "you wouldn't dream of cleaning your body by just wiping it with paper!"

A Saudi commentator put the issue succinctly:

> Westerners consider us dirty for touching our mess but we can't understand how people can walk around with a butt full of manure. They do realize it though; when a pretty girl wears a G-string bikini, they say she is flossing! But hygiene is hygiene and that's all there is to it.

If we were all as honest as the main character in Philip Roth's *Portnoy's Complaint* we would agree. On the psychiatrist's couch, filled with guilt, he reveals the sins of his youth. Although I wipe and wipe "until that little orifice of mine is red as a raspberry" there always remains that telltale "pale and wispy brush-stroke of shit in the seam of my undershorts."

Philip Roth's youthful self would have been spared this humiliation had butt washing been part of his culture. He also may have been spared considerable discomfort later in life.

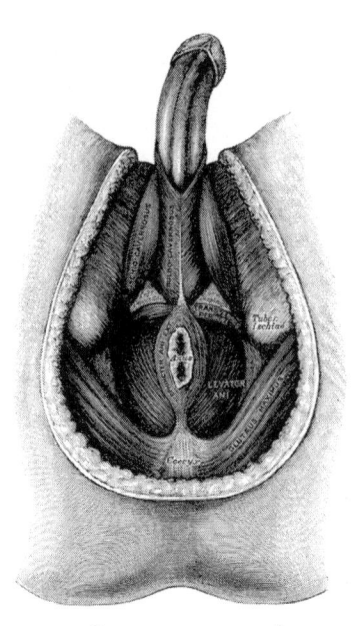

The perineum—the area of our anatomy between the anus and the vagina or penis—is a region with very delicate membranes and protective mucosa. If we abuse it, as we frequently do, it will exact revenge on us with pain or a condition called in doctor code, *pruritus ani*—ani = Latin for anus, pruritus = Latin for itch. Given the extreme sensitivity of this area of the body, it is the sort of itch that can, and does, drive people to distraction.

> *Who with the leaves shall wipe at need*
> *The place, where swelling piles breed:*
> *May every ill, that bites, or smarts,*
> *Perplex him in his hinder-parts*
>
> Robert Herrick (1591-1674)

It is an itch with many causes. It can be an allergic reaction. In the days of newspaper wiping, printer's ink was the culprit. A doctor questioning an agonized patient one hundred years ago discovered that the frugal man was using the thin paper that oranges were once wrapped in. The man's anal area had hives either from the printing on the paper or the zest from the orange peels. Color-coordinated toilet paper with certain dyes, introduced in the 1930s, had a similar effect on some particularly sensitive rears. When a nutty marketer in the 1970s introduced perfumed toilet paper, doctors' offices filled with sweet smelling but itchy anuses. The stuff has now been banned.

Nowadays a leading cause is excessive wiping, which at least irritates the skin and at worst can actually abrade it. Some people obsessively over-clean the area with harsh soap, robbing the membranes of their natural oils. But the most common cause of anal itch are those dreaded entities always referred to in the painful plural— hemorrhoids.

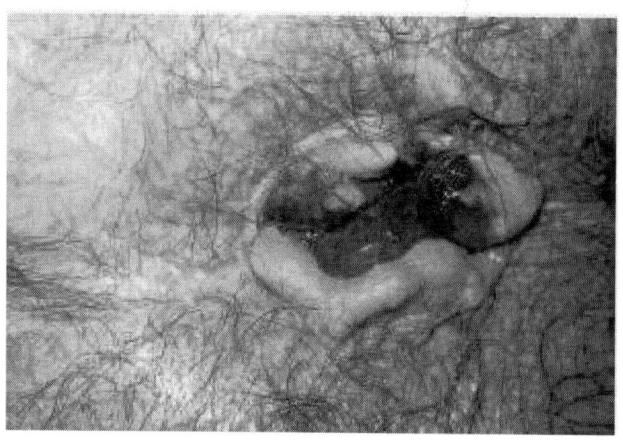

Hemorrhoids are swollen veins in the anus, and if the condition worsens, these veins can protrude out from the rectum causing untold misery. Napoleon had them so badly he couldn't ride a horse. Historians debate whether piles caused him to lose the Battle of Waterloo. Jimmy Carter had surgery in 1982 for his condition, and Ernest Hemingway had to skip a few bull fights because of his rectal distress. As noted before, it is the most common ailment known to man and even more to women. Most of the human race suffers from this condition sometime in their lives and it seems to have tortured the tails of the human race ever since we walked on two legs. In fact they are a consequence of our walking on two legs and putting the full force of gravity on the pelvic region.

The Bible is full of hemorrhoids, as in Psalm 78:66: "And he smote his enemies in the hinder parts: he put them to a perpetual reproach" and in Deuteronomy 28 Moses warns his people: "If you do not obey the Lord your God and do not carefully follow all his commands... The Lord will smite thee with the botch of Egypt, and with the emerods, and with the scab, and with the itch, whereof thou canst not be healed." The God of the Old Testament did not mess around with his smites.

Hippocrates (460-377 BCE), known as the father of medicine, recommended goose grease for mild cases of hemorrhoids. For the severe cases he had a remedy that no patient was likely to forget:

> Having laid the patient on his back, and placing a pillow below the breech, force out the anus as much as possible with the fingers, and make the irons red-hot, and burn the pile until it be dried up so as that no part may be left behind. And burn so as to leave none of the hemorrhoids unburnt, for you should burn them all up. You will recognize the hemorrhoids without difficulty, for they project on the inside of the gut like dark-colored grapes, and when the anus is forced out they spurt blood. When the iron is applied the patient's head and hands should be held so that he may not stir, but he himself should cry out, for this will make the rectum project the more. When you have performed the burning, boil lentils and tares, and apply as a cataplasm for five or six days.

And you thought you had problems.

The modern procedure is called hemorrhoidectomy and it is a bit more pleasant and most cases can be managed without surgery. The fact remains that, rubbing external hemorrhoids with dry toilet paper, no matter how soft and fluffy, will only irritate the condition. French proctologist Guy Benhamou predicts the coming of a third hygienic revolution. According to the good doctor, after having learned to wash our hands and clean our teeth, we will soon all be bathing our anuses. The ASCRS (The American Society of Colon and Rectal Surgeons) also recommends washing, not wiping after defecation, for America's many sufferers of hemorrhoids.

If anyone is counting, in the contest between washers and wipers, the score is now: washers 3, wipers 0.

As seen earlier in our discussion of Muslim bathroom rituals, many people in the world have mastered the complex task of cleaning their butts with their left hand while pouring water from a pitcher held with their right hand. The teapot-like pitcher used to perform this operation has gained iconic significance in Bangladesh and Pakistan, where it is called a *bodna*.

There is great affection for this device even though it is disappearing from some modern homes. This nostalgia is movingly captured in the popular Bangladeshi music video with the catchy title *Bodna Nai* (No Bodna). Here we watch the singer pining, not for his lost love, but for the lost pitcher of his youth.

No bodna... aah aah aah!
Today's toilet what is there?
With them how butt clean happen?

In hotels and modern homes, the *bodna* of the young man's yearnings has been replaced with a hose device installed beside the toilet. It has also been dubbed 'The Islamic Shower'.

For $44.95 on Amazon you can buy a device discretely called a 'Multi-Use Hand Held Sprayer Kit' which can be easily installed on any toilet. To a non-practitioner like myself however, it would seem to be as difficult to use as the *bodna*. The trick would be to wipe and spray while avoiding projecting excrement onto the walls and ceiling.

Fortunately, for the less mechanically dexterous among us, there is the bidet.

The word 'bidet' comes from the French word for pony because, in its use, you sit astride it like riding a pony. It was the invention of French furniture makers and became the appliance *de rigueur* of every aristocratic boudoir of the 18th century. Madame Du Barry had one with inlaid wood and a silver bowl, Madame de

Pompadour had a bidet with a back of rosewood. Its feet and trim were made of gold-plated bronze and it featured a hand-operated spray pump to shoot the water right up there. Cost: 300 Louis d'or or about 800 times the annual wages of the average French peasant.

The bidet is a wonderful invention, allowing the user to sit in the nice warm water and clean what is affectionately called 'the beast,' the smelliest, dirtiest part of our anatomy, pleasantly and effectively. At first it was used by women for front and back cleaning, but men soon realized its utility and began to sit astride the instrument as well.

Unfortunately for British and American perineums, this fine instrument only really caught on in France. A common appliance in brothels for obvious reasons, this perfectly respectable cleaning device got a bad reputation. The British considered it highly immoral and Americans tourists coming on it in their hotel bathroom couldn't for the life of them figure out what the darn thing was for and ended up using it to wash their socks.

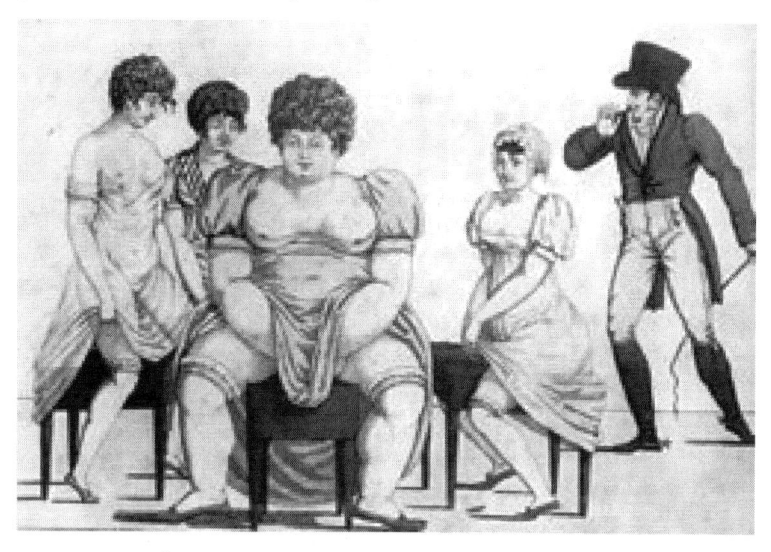

In the early 20th century, bidets became a common appliance in French homes. Their success was due to a heightened concern with butt cleanliness perhaps because the laundry, at least in Paris, was no longer done by servants at home but was sent out to the neighborhood *blanchisserie*. For this reason French men and women, like Portnoy, became very self-conscious about that tell-tale brown stain left deposited on one's underwear by an improperly cleaned bum. In recent years, with French homes having a bathtub or a shower as well as a washing machine, the bidet is disappearing. But this, the most effective anal cleaning device ever invented, would rise again on the other side of the world and in a most surprising form.

Traditionally, the Japanese were wipers, or more specifically scrapers because they used rough sticks. Although a culture that valued cleanliness, they were not very fussy about their toilets, particularly the public ones which, according to Rose George, were often described by the four K's: kiken (dangerous) kitanain (dirty) kurai (dark) and kasia (stinky).

Japan has a tradition of sudden and enormous technological leaps. In the 19th century, they went from a feudal society to an industrial superpower in one generation. The same is true with their toilets. From using filthy squat holes in the floor, they leapfrogged to toilets for the space age. Devices made by TOTO and other Japanese companies combine the normal function of a toilet with that of a high-tech bidet.

Washlet E200

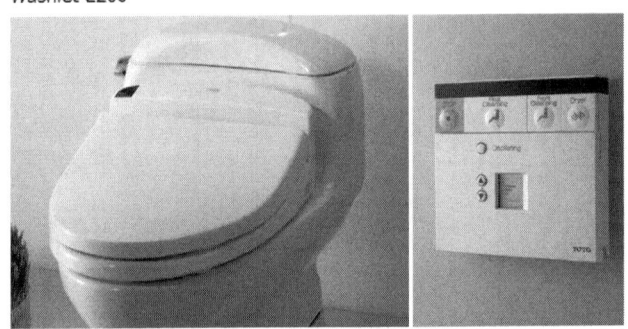

After defecating but without getting up from the seat, the user presses a button, and warm water is squirted precisely at the anus but at a carefully calculated angle so that the stool adhering to the buttocks will fall into the toilet bowl. After this operation is complete, a jet of warm air dries the orifice.

Warm Water Wash

Warm Air Dryer

These high-tech devices can be fine-tuned to the personal preferences as to the duration of the wash and the temperature of the water, resulting in a perfectly clean, dry butt, untouched by human hands. All models feature a self-cleaning nozzle, and what is discretely termed front and rear cleaning. And that is just the no-frills model. Other units feature heated seats, an automatic flush, an auto seat raiser and lowerer (for the men of the house), an air purifier, a pulsating spray (for those stubborn dingleberries), and a wireless remote control. Suddenly the roll of paper looks as primitive as we regard the sticks, stones and sponges of ages gone by.

In Japan, over one million of these devices are sold each year. It is said that more households own a 'Washlet' than own a computer. You would think these wonderfully engineered devices would be sweeping the world— particularly gadget-hungry America. TOTO launched a 'clean is happy' campaign several years ago in an attempt to sell their units to Americans. They even set-up a demonstration model in New York's busy Times Square.

> We think outside the bowl.
> Motto of USABIDET

TOTO bidet toilets have been installed in fancy restaurants and high-priced hotels, but to date they have made only the slightest impression on American rear ends. "The toilet is the last bastion that has not been luxurified," says Janice Costa, the editor of *Kitchen & Bath Design News*. With everything in our world changing at an alarming rate, perhaps the toilet is the last seat of tradition.

If we have learned anything in this history, it is that people are extremely conservative about their toilet rituals. Change comes slowly, if at all. It took a great effort to move us from newspaper to toilet paper, and the British were content to use a brand of toilet paper not much softer than newspaper for most of the last century.

In 2001 Kimberly Clark's invested 100 million dollars to invent and market a new system that would dispense moistened toilet paper on a roll. It was an excellent idea and a great product, but 'Cottonelle Fresh Rollwipes' were a massive flop. Americans are determinately not going to let water anywhere near their rear ends while on the toilet.

The moral of the story is the tautology that—we are used to what we are used to. Just as there are no absolutes in bodily cleanliness—it's a cultural thing—so there are no absolutes in anal cleanliness. Many of us are perfectly happy to go through life, as that Saudi so graphically put it, "with a butt full of manure," others insist on absolutely immaculate asses extending right into the anus. The truth is that we shall wipe or wash or scrape or dab as we always have. But mainly, we will avoid talking or thinking about this subject at all.

For most of us with a healthy perineum and a strong immune system, our own bathroom rituals and those of others, whatever they may be, do not have to be of great concern. But the topic is not a trivial one. For some people in the world, how we wipe can be, in a literal not a metaphorical sense, a matter of life and death.

THE BOTTOM LINE

If talking about defecation is taboo, the subject of this study has proven to be even more taboo. With all our supposed sophistication, we cannot seem to deal with this subject except with a smirk and a giggle. In millions of personal blogs on the Internet in which individuals freely and often shamelessly reveal to the world the most intimate details of their everyday lives, they choose to omit this, the commonest activity of everyday life. As detailed before, even the movies, which glory in shocking and disgusting people, find this one topic just a little too shocking and disgusting. Advertisers pussyfoot around the subject with clouds, babies, and bears. Bidet marketers cannot market because they cannot come out and trumpet what their product does so well. We reserve this subject for our smuttiest jokes or our nastiest epithets. If we want to show an object or idea the greatest contempt imaginable, we actually or symbolically wipe our ass with it.

But like everything taboo, what surprised me in researching this topic is the great underground interest in the subject. When I shook this particular tree of knowledge the forbidden fruit came falling down in surprising quantities. There is a lot on the Internet about this subject if you know where to look. (See appendix.) Everyone seems to have a story on the subject, most notably tourists coming back from places with, in their eyes, exotic bathroom etiquettes. But the topic is certainly not part of the mainstream media. You never read in someone's autobiography a proud reference to their contributions to the science of anal cleaning. Large corporations making huge profits from the sale of toilet paper downplay the topic in their annual reports and corporate histories. None of this is surprising. There is still a deep-seated shame in anything connected with the subject of our bottoms. There is, however, a price to be paid for this avoidance, and that is the real shame.

Squeamishness about discussing or dealing with the subject of anal cleaning is odd but understandable in every group of people except one—the medical profession. Doctors know that what is clinically referred to as the 'fecal-oral route' remains a major cause of human misery, disease, and death in much of the world. According to the World Health Organization, in 2002, almost two million people died from acute infectious diarrheal diseases, most of them young children. Much of this terrible carnage is due to fecally contaminated water, but some of it is also be due to contaminated hands touching food. As we have seen from Dr. Phillip Tierno's swabbing of New York door handles, even in cleanliness-obsessed America, we come in daily contact with microscopic quantities of human shit.

The reason that all of us are not sick all of the time is because, for most of us, contact with human excrement is completely harmless. (There are even arguments that exposure to the bacteria is good for us. It keeps our immune system busy preventing it from turning inward and causing a variety of autoimmune diseases such as rheumatoid arthritis.) The problem is that contact with the excrement of our neighbors and co-workers is only harmless until it is not harmless.

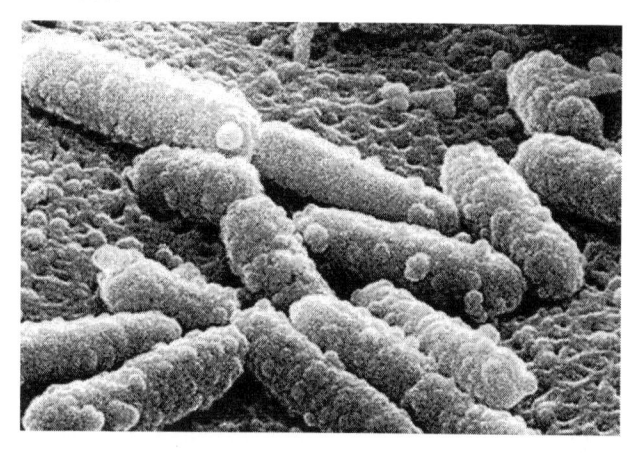

In all, 70 species of bacteria has been isolated from human feces and (since this too is a shockingly neglected topic of research) the number 70 is a tiny fraction of the flora and fauna in our guts. Thankfully, most of these organisms are benign, but human stool can contain serious pathogens including bacteroides, specie salmonella and shigella yersinia campylobacter, aeromonas, candida, E. coli O157, cryptosporidium, entamoeba histolytica, all potentially bad news if ingested. And that's just the small stuff. Excrement also contains the cysts and eggs of worms and single-celled parasites that if ingested can cause mild, to violent, to deadly diarrhea, to chronic fatigue, malnourishment, and immune dysfunction. A recent study conducted in Nepal found that 71% of the children tested were infected with intestinal parasites[65].

And then we have the major killers: dysentery, typhoid, and the horror of all these horrors—cholera. The cholera bacillus developed the ability to survive a long time in water and in the strong acids of our stomach juices. Once ingested, this terrifying disease produces violent vomiting, diarrhea, fever and, if untreated, death within a few hours of the first symptoms. In the 19th century, it killed 13% of the population of Cairo and then went on to decimate the population of every major city in Europe. And the microbe's deadly legacy lives on. In 2009, cholera sickened about 4 million people and killed over 100,000.

The United States, where drinking water is presumably shit-free, reports 150 million cases of acute diarrheal episodes a year. Some of this illness is caused by the ingestion of fecally contaminated food. So how does excrement get from butts to hands to our food? Obviously the only time we come in contact with the stuff is when we are wiping or washing our rears after defecation. And given that many of these microbes can survive outside of the body only for several hours, the shit we and others transmit when making sandwiches, touching elevator buttons, door knobs, subway poles, and shaking hands with friends and neighbors, is fresh shit. There is a good reason for that sign posted in the bathroom of every restaurant. Food handlers must indeed wash their hands after defecation, but the very fact that the sign is necessary is indicative of the fact that they do not do it. For people with a healthy immune system, this isn't much of a problem. The situation is more serious in hospitals, where study after study shows that doctors, nurses, and aides do not wash their hands properly. For extremely sick people with compromised immune systems, that microscopic bit of shit under the fingernails can, and all too often does, kill.

With this exception, for most people in Western countries, fecal contamination remains a relatively minor problem. In developing countries it is a different story. In much of the world, millions of people suffer from fecal-oral illness and billions of others in the world suffer from a chronic infestation of one or more of the feces-caused infestations. The results are malnourishment, vulnerability to other diseases, and sometimes death.

Health workers have put the numbers in these dramatic terms; it is as if one jumbo jet plane carrying mainly children blows up and crashes killing everyone on board *every two hours*. That is how many people die each year from illness traveling the fecal-oral route. Most of this death and illness is due to poor sanitation—few or no toilets, resulting in water contaminated with human waste. But again, some fraction of this horror is caused by dirty hands—hands dirtied in the act of anal cleaning. How exactly this act is performed is critical to our health and the health of those we touch. You would think that when and how we come into direct contact with our feces during anal cleaning would be a focus of medical research.

You would think…

All of the papers I have read on the subject repeat the same message; 'isn't it shocking that there is no serious research in this area?' Dr Walter T. Hughes, an expert in infectious disease, writes: "In modern use, toilet paper would seem to play an important role as a barrier to the transmission of enteric infection by the fecal-manual-oral route. A historical review reveals a dearth of information on this topic. The remarkable compliance with the hygienic practice of toilet paper use is in contrast to the more limited compliance with hand-washing policies touted universally as a sound infection-control measure."[66] He reports that during World War One, the incidence of typhoid fever—a terrible disease taking the now familiar fecal-oral route—afflicted three soldiers per thousand. He notes that this disease has been effectively eliminated today. "What role did toilet paper have in the control of this and other diseases?" asks Dr. Hughes, "clearly, no one knows or will ever know." This is simply not a subject that has been studied. "Despite the lack of evidence for the role of toilet paper in the prevention of diseases, our general knowledge of microbial diseases leads us to expect that the use of toilet paper has served a preventive function."

But is toilet paper really effective in this respect? A complete survey of the literature on the diseases linked to this particular fecal-oral route retrieves few papers on this subject. A very small study in Burma in 1985 showed that the use of toilet paper, as opposed to anal washing, cut down on the spread of dysentery.[67] Another small study in Burundi in 1997 links the reuse of cloth rags for anal cleaning with dysentery, which in turn is the cause of 10% of all deaths in that country.[68] And just to prove that a seemingly insignificant change in wiping habits can have an enormous health benefit, the British Medical Journal reported a study done on his own by a Doctor R.E.W. Fisher linking the use of hard versus soft toilet paper in two children's institutions with the prevalence of dysentery. He found "an important change in community hygiene" with a lower incidence of the disease with the use of soft toilet paper, perhaps because of its "superior cleaning power."[69]

This survey of the few articles written on the subject demonstrates that this is indeed a legitimate field of research but the lack of study in this area should no longer surprise us. This is the real-world price of our refusal to deal with the subject—the cost of denial. Any researcher who might want to do such a study would have to apply for a grant from a funding agency. You can imagine the scene: "Okay committee, next we have the application from Mr. Smith who wants $50,000 to do a study on ass wiping. How do you think that will play in Congress?" After much merriment around the room Mr. Smith's application is rejected. It may be a stretch to say that such studies might save lives, but the questions are certainly worth asking.

And so many questions remain: does toilet paper give us a false sense of security even though it is, in fact, transparent to bacteria? Do we fail to wash our hands properly because, after using toilet paper, we think our hands are germ free? Do the anal washers of the world have cleaner hands because they have touched their excrement and therefore feel it necessary to scrub their hands thoroughly? Or is anal washing inherently worse in this respect than wiping?

Considering the billions of dollars spent on medical research in all the thousands of laboratories around the world you would think that the World Health Organization and the National Institutes of Health in the United States and other countries would be spending at least some small amount of money to research these basic questions. You would think that among the thousands of studies about everything that affects humanity from pimples to erectile dysfunction, there would be at least some controlled studies of this subject.

You would think…

I began this research knowing that this is a subject which is either ignored or handled with embarrassed humor. I did not realize that because of this twisted attitude to a normal bodily function, the shame we feel has serious global health consequences.

Researchers know that it is often the simple, low-tech solutions that have a real impact on people's health. Netting to prevent malaria is more important to most of the world's population than are MRI machines. Hand-operated pumps to supply clean water will save more lives than will expensive drugs. Exercise and diet is more effective than are expensive drugs in preventing heart disease. Could it be that giving out toilet paper and encouraging its use could have a major impact on the health of the world? Could it be that supplying the world with bidets would have an even greater effect? To quote Dr. Hughes again, "clearly, no one knows," and because of our bizarre collective refusal to deal directly with this simple everyday routine, we probably never will.

10
TP STATS & FOLLIES

Modern toilet paper production.
Thousands of individual rolls are cut from each
of these so-called mother rolls.

In 2010 the world wiped away 28,300,000 metric tons of toilet paper.[70] This number is so staggering that we must spread it out on a spreadsheet, starting with the world's biggest wipers, Americans:

SHEETS OF TP PER AMERICAN PER DAY	577
SHEETS USED PER YEAR	20,805
INCHES IN A SHEET	4
ACTIVE WIPING POPULATION	250,000,000
INCHES USED PER YEAR	9,005,403,160,125
INCHES IN A MILE	63,360
MILES OF TP USED PER YEAR	142,130,732
DISTANCE EARTH TO THE MOON	238,875
NUMBER OF TRIPS TO THE MOON IN TP	595

This is a conservative calculation[71]. Americans each use on the average 20,805 sheets of toilet paper a year at 4 inches a sheet. The population of the United States is well over 310 million but I have chosen the lower figure of 250 million to discount for newborns at one end and those wearing a colostomy bag at the other end. With the spreadsheet doing the adding and dividing, we come up with the astounding figure that if `all the toilet paper Americans used were unrolled end to end, the paper would stretch to the moon <u>and back</u> a bit under three hundred times.

All these trips to the moon and back are riding on U.S. toilet paper usage only. If we include the world's growing usage of this product and extend the numbers out for a few years, the long arm of bathroom tissue will soon reach the inner planets and someday beyond.

Greenpeace has an ongoing campaign against this wasteful practice of ours, pointing out that we flush one out of every seven trees harvested down the drain. As usual, they know how to catch the eye of the press when urging the rears of America to buy and use only TP made with recycled paper

How exactly do we wipe with toilet paper? Paper companies have detailed statistics of this nature locked in their most secure vaults. They calculate how many sheets/shit we use by a complex formula using the following variables:

S = the speed of transit
A = the anatomy of the individual's buttocks, specifically the depth of the intergluteal cleft: deeper = more paper; shallower = less
C = the consistency of the stool: harder = less paper; softer = more.

It is probably easier to extract the secrets of bomb building from the Pentagon than to get the huge corporations who now monopolize this industry to make public such intriguing information. But one intrepid researcher, Paul Spinrad, did an informal survey on his own with Californian college students.[72] According to his figures, the members of his sample used 5.90 sheets per tear and 3.23 tears per loaf (as he puts it). He goes deeper into the subject and comes up with these fascinating facts:

42% of people fold the paper.

33% crumple it.

8% a little of both and the rest say it depends on their mood.

44% wipe front to back, 11% back to front.

38% moisten the paper for improved cleaning.

58% (mostly women) remain seated while wiping.

60% (mostly men) examine the paper after each wipe.

Another survey reports that if you are 35 years or older you are more likely to tear along the perforations. The young and reckless are more likely to tear randomly.

Now that toilet paper has gone global the prolific French author Martin Monestier commented on the cross-cultural trends in wiping. Americans, he claimed, tend to dab, the British rub back and forth while Germans wipe extremely vigorously and therefore prefer very strong toilet paper with large sheets. The French do a gentler swipe and therefore prefer smaller, thinner sheets. He decried the tendency of the increasing standardization of sheet size resulting in, "une sorte d'égalité devant la merde" and cited this as yet another example of evil American hegemony.

THE GREAT DEBATE

And now that age-old debate, which has divided friends, families, troubled marriages, and has provoked more than one fight in a bar ever since Seth Wheeler first introduced his product to the world: what is the 'right' way to install a roll of toilet paper—over or under?

UNDER 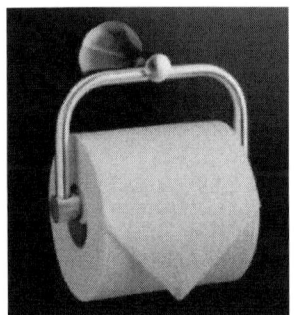   OVER

Arguments on this subject rage in books, on TV, and on the Internet. Ann Landers, of newspaper advice column fame, once dared to opine on this question and received 15,000 letters making this the most controversial issue in her column's 31-year history. If you do a Google search putting the words 'toilet paper orientation' in quotes you get, as of May 2011, 50,927 hits. In one survey of Americans, 60% say over, 29% say under and an apathetic 7% just don't care.[73] But that is just one survey. Much more detailed surveys, including those breaking the numbers down by age and sex and earned income, can be found in Wikipedia's 1000-word article discussing every possible aspect of this riveting subject, backed up with 127 footnotes and a page of 'further readings.'

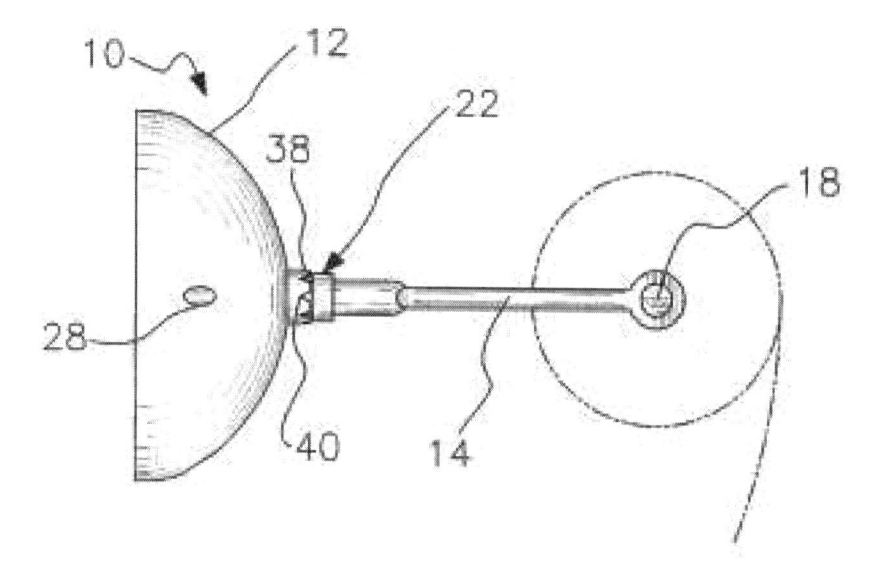

Proving that there is a technological fix to even the most intractable of human conflicts, Curtis Batts, a Dallas industrial engineer has invented the 'Tilt-a-Roll' dispenser — US patent numbers 5588615 and 5690302, described in his patent abstract as: "a rotatable paper roll holder for rotatably supporting a roll of paper for dispensing of the paper either from over or from under the roll."

Because we are inherently crazy, cretinous, creative creatures, the human race just could not leave this innocent product alone to perform its useful function in peace. That is not the human way. For one thing, there is so much of the stuff around—it is so available. Also, given its use and our attitude to its use, it is too charged with symbolism and meaning. Doing things with TP is just too tempting.

And it *is* paper. Back in 1857, Mr. Gayetty was so proud to offer the public an ass wipe free of printer's ink. So what do we do…?

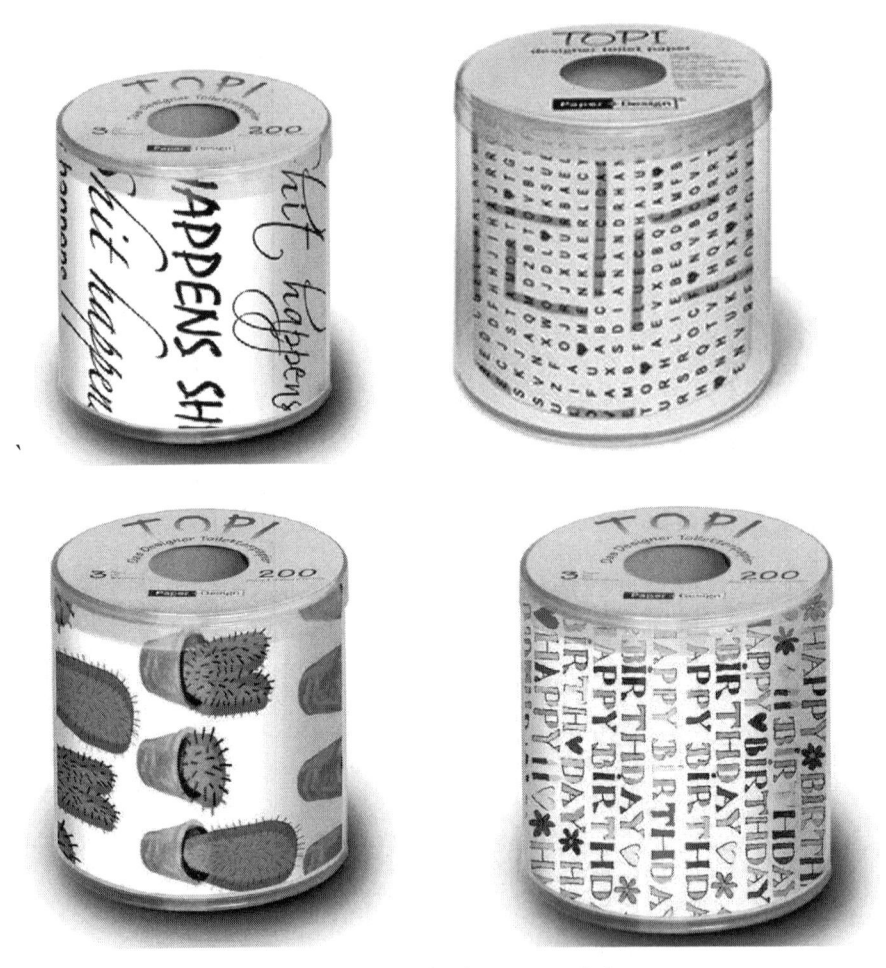

For these and other designer models go to
www.ChristmasToiletPaper.com

And like everything else, how could toilet paper fail to be political? No sooner does a candidate manage to stick his or her head above the fray than it becomes raw material to stick up their opponents' rears.

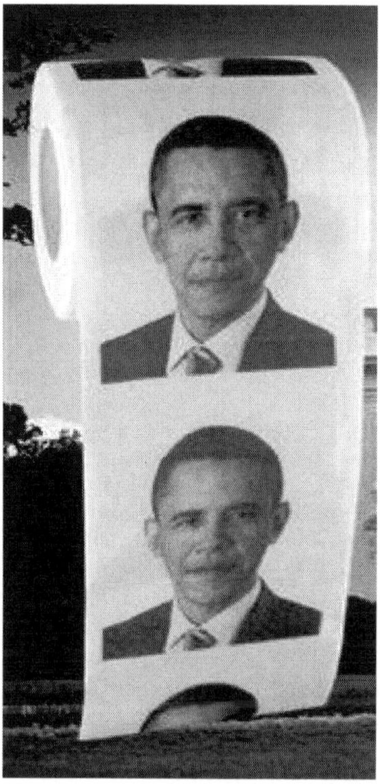

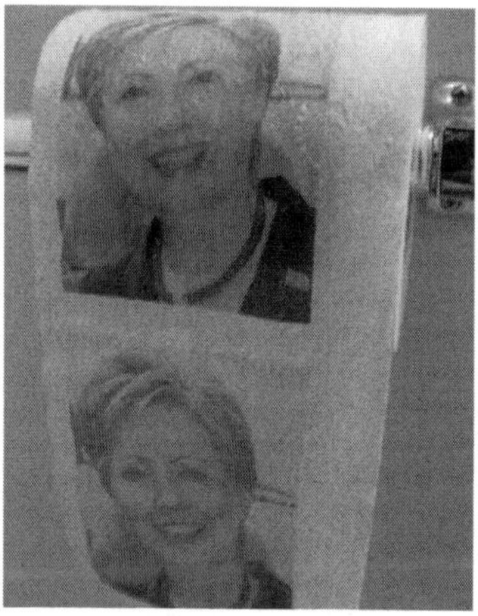

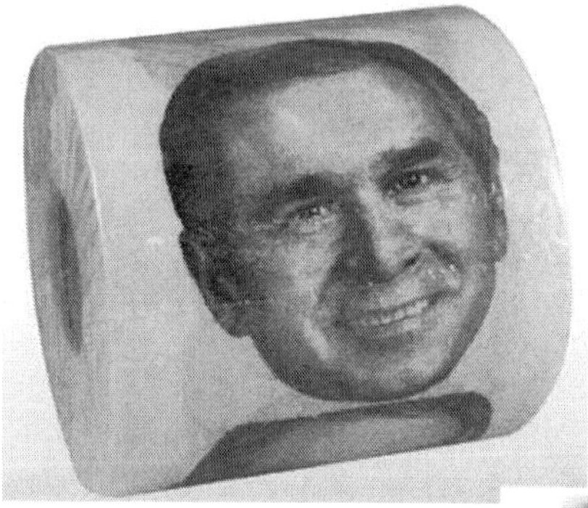

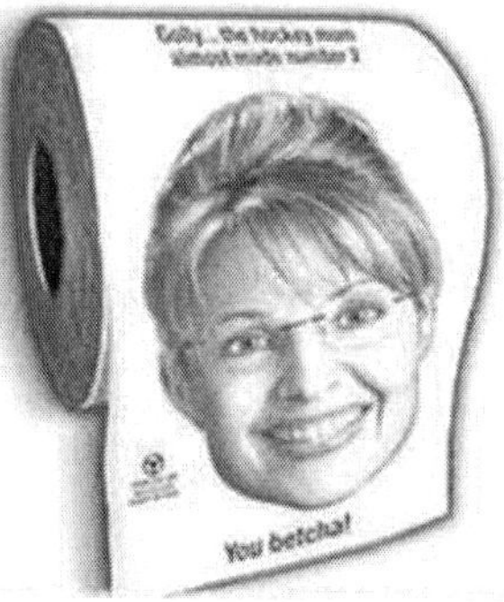
You betcha!

Just to show that there is nothing new under the bum, here is a real collector's item—the image from a sheet of World War Two patriotic toilet paper:

"NOW I'M BROWNSHIRT ALL OVER"

After the war, the East Germans carried on this tradition by printing English lessons on their toilet paper, combining both pedagogy with politics.

As noted earlier, the British now not only collect printed toilet paper but have invented a new word for this hobby: '*cloacopapyrology*'. They have an edge on Americans because, as we have seen, until the 1990s they used so-called hard toilet paper, which is so much easier to print on than is the squishy American stuff. And print on it they did.

Imagine, if you will, a stormy night in London, and a meeting of British cloacopapyrologists as they pore over their collections with powerful magnifying glasses, singing praises when someone produces the rare piece with sans serif typeface or print of an unusual font color. Cheers would rise around the room when someone reveals a previously unnoticed watermark.

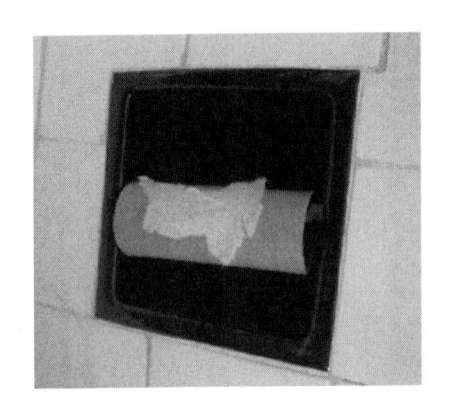

ENDPAPER

As a film maker I have been admonished always to remember what is called 'the holy shit list.' This is a technical term. It refers to an important reality: over the months or years that it can take to produce a film, we can often forget or bury the exciting facts that we have uncovered during the research. Film makers are therefore reminded to write down those aspects of the subject that they find exciting when first discovered and remember to include them in the final film. The mantra goes something like this: 'when people at a dinner party ask you to describe what you are working on, what is the first thing you tell them?' With this project I have been very frustrated at dinner parties because, whenever I tried to describe what I was working on, most people nervously changed the subject. I did however retain my holy shit list and since you, dear reader, have managed to soldier on with me, I have saved the best for the last.

There was a moment in time when ass wiping altered the course of history and even more the career of one man. The story is told in the now-classic *Memoirs of le Duc de Saint-Simon* in which he gives us the great behind-the-scenes gossip from inside the Court of Louis XIV.

It begins with this haughty looking gentleman. Louis Joseph de Bourbon, Duke of Vendôme (1654 –1712). Of royal, if illegitimate blood, the grandson of a union of Henry IV of France and his mistress, Vendôme was extremely wealthy and France's most able military commander in a time of almost continual European wars. In his personal habits, however, he was one of the most revolting human beings who ever lived. He would sleep with his dogs and was delighted when one of them gave birth in his bed, ignoring the mess. He ate huge quantities of food, not caring much about its freshness, and when he encountered a particularly rotten piece of fish, he would vomit it out in front of his dinner guests and then go on eating. Like his patron, the Sun King, he would receive visitors while defecating on his close-stool, but that was perhaps the least offensive part of his behavior as documented by Saint-Simone:

> M. de Vendôme (and I report only the bare unvarnished facts) arrived at Ghent between 7 and 8 o'clock in the morning as his troops were entering the town. He stopped with his entourage, dismounted, let down his breeches, and there and then planted his stools right beside the troops as they paraded past him.[74]

In 1706 the French army was fighting the Austrians in the Italian principality of Parma, and the Duke of Parma rightly feared that, when the soldiers were finished battling one another, they would do what all 18th century armies did— rape and ravage the surrounding countryside. The Duke of Parma, who maintained a position of neutrality in this conflict, determined to ask Vendôme to move the battle out of town.

Vendôme, as well as being a boor, was erratic and capricious and therefore a very difficult man with whom to negotiate. In an attempt to awe this royal bastard, the Duke decided to send the Bishop of Parma. Dressed in his purple clerical robes he was received by Vendôme sitting on his close-stool. Surprised, but always the diplomat, the Bishop began to discuss the terms of a potential treaty. Vendôme finished his bowel movement, slowly got up from the close-stool, turned around so that the dignified elderly gentleman would be exposed to a full view of his rear end, and then slowly and methodically began to wipe himself. This was too much for the Bishop.

> He immediately turned around and went back to Parma saying that nothing on earth would induce him to have anything more do with such a horror.[75]

All would have been lost for the potential rape-ees and pillage-ees of Parma if it hadn't been for the brilliance and unrequited ambition of Abbé Alberoni, the humble son of a gardener whom the Duke next sent to try and deal with this ornery nobleman.

This low-ranking cleric was received by Vendôme as he was again performing his morning business. The Abbé resumed the negotiations. Predictably Vendôme listened with amusement then, on cue, slowly got up, pushed his exposed lower anatomy into the face of the cleric and began to wipe. The Abbé knew that this was his moment. He cried out in mock joy, "*O culo di angelo!*" (Oh, the ass of an angel!) and bent over to kiss each cheek of Vendôme's ample rear end. The Duke was so totally delighted by this action that not only did he agree to negotiate with the Italian prince (making Alberoni a hero back in Parma), but on the spot he appointed this wonderfully versatile Abbé to be his personal assistant.

In 1711, Alberoni accompanied Vendôme to Spain where the French were supporting the candidacy of the future Philip V to the Spanish throne. After Philip was crowned king, he rewarded the Abbé with a dukedom for his diplomatic efforts and soon appointed Alberoni to be his Prime Minister.

This was only the beginning of his rise to power. In 1715, Alberoni was ordained a cardinal by the Pope, the second most powerful post in the Catholic Church, and in 1724 he came several votes short of being elected Pope himself. He was an able administrator and very successful businessman and, according to the Catholic Encyclopedia, he exhibited talents and abilities very much ahead of his time. When this supreme diplomat died in 1754, however, the official biographies failed to mention this first crucial step in his meteoric rise to wealth and power: the wipe that launched his world.

Cardinal Alberoni

ABOUT THE AUTHOR

Ronald Blumer has written/produced/or co-produced over eighty documentary films, including three series with Bill Moyers, *Creativity, a Walk thru the 20th Century, & The U.S. Constitution*. For PBS, he has written & co-produced the six-part series, *Liberty! The American Revolution,* a three-part miniseries on the life of *Benjamin Franklin,* & *American Photography, A Century Of Images,* & he co-wrote an episode of Ric Burns' *New York*. His other writing credits include: a program about the 1929 stock market crash for *The American Exp*erience; the PBS series', *Dancing;* & *Discovering Women*; the Turner Broadcasting series, *Portrait of America*; a one hour dramatic film, *An Empire of Reason*, on the ratification of the Constitution; & the Audio version of *Iaccoca* for Bantam Books. His script for the National Film Board's *Paperland,* won the Canadian Film Academy's award for best non-fiction script. He wrote treatments for a six hour dramatic series on the life of Prime Minister Mackenzie King for the Canadian Broadcasting Corporation, & for PBS's four hour special on the life of Lyndon Johnson. He worked on the design and scripted interactive exhibits for the National Constitution Center in Philadelphia, & interactives for the traveling exhibit 'Benjamin Franklin: In Search of a Better World,' & a video on the history of the First Amendment for the Newseum in Washington, D.C. He wrote a Nova special, *Saving The National Treasures*, about the re-encasement of the founding documents & a film on the Mariinsky Theater, *The Sacred Stage,* which premiered at the Kennedy Center.

In 2006 he wrote the two part PBS series *The New Medicine*. The PBS two-hour program on the life of Alexander Hamilton was nominated for a Writer's Guild Award in 2008, as was *Dolley Madison* in 2011. His work has received thirty major awards including four Emmy awards & a George Foster Peabody.

As a writer/journalist, he was Contributing Editor to the film magazines, *Take One*, & *Cinema Canada*. He was film critic on the morning radio program of the CBC. His articles have been anthologized in various books & publications including film program notes for the Museum of Modern Art. He has written a book about the film director Donald Brittain, & co-authored the companion book to *The New Medicine*. He taught documentary film research & writing at New York University's Film School.

INTERNET SITES

There are surprisingly many internet sites devoted to the various aspects of anal cleaning. Some are well researched and some are filled with facts that are the products of their authors' imagination which are then repeated on other sites. What follows are some recommendations:

An excellent trade magazine:
http://www.tissueworldmagazine.com
British toilet paper collecting society:
http://www.ephemera-society.org.uk/articles/cloacopapyrology.html
For a history of early toilets:
http://www.sewerhistory.org/grfx/privbath/toilet1.htm
Blog by Dave Praeger describing his experiments with pre-paper wiping techniques
http://www.poopreport.com/Techniques/Content/Wiping/wipingbc.html
Transcript of WJT's discussion of how to advertise Scott TP
http://library.duke.edu/digitalcollections/mma_MM1156/
Historical ads for TP and various sanitary products.
http://library.duke.edu/digitalcollections/mma.MM0583/pg.1/
World statistics for the 30 billion dollar TP industry.
http://www.aeos.cn/En/Info/Html/2008-7/Info_6_15245519.html
News about world sanitary projects:
http://sanitationupdates.wordpress.com/
Early cistern studies in Japan:
http://www.scielo.br/pdf/mioc/v98s1/v98s1a19.pdf
Power Point on Islamic anal cleaning:
http://wn.com/Islamic_toilet_etiquette
WHO pamphlet on Islamic sanitary practices:
http://www.emro.who.int/dsaf/dsa114.pdf
Wikipedia entries:
http://en.wikipedia.org/wiki/Islamic_toilet_etiquette
http://en.wikipedia.org/wiki/Toilet_paper_orientation
Google US Patent Search engine
http://www.google.com/patents

BIBLIOGRAPHY

Al-Sheikh, Abdul Fattah. *Water and Sanitation in Islam.* Alexandria, Egypt: World Health Organization, 1996.

Bourke, John. *The Portable Scatalog.* New York: William Morrow, 1994.

Clarke, John R. "Look Who's Laughing: Humor In Tavern Painting," *Memoirs of the American Academy in Rome*, vols. 43/44 (1998/1999): 27-48.

Cohen, Elizabeth S., and Cohen, Thomas V. *Daily Life in Renaissance Italy.* Westport, CT: Greenwood Press, 2001.

Eveleigh, David J. *Privies & Water Closets.* Oxford, UK: Shire Books, 2010.

Gatrell, Vic. *City of Laughter: Sex and Satire in Eighteenth-Century London.* New York: Walker & Co., 2006.

George, Rose. *The Big Necessity: The Unmentionable World of Human Waste and Why It Matters.* New York: Henry Holt, 2008.

Great Britain: Office of the Commissioners of Patents for Inventions. *Patents for Inventions: Abridgments of Specifications.* London: Printed by George E. Eyre and William Spottiswoode / Published at the Office of the Commissioners of Patents for Inventions, (1878-1885).

Henderson, Jeffrey. *The Maculate Muse: Obscene Language in Attic Comedy*, second edition. New York: Oxford University Press, 1991.

Horan, Julie L. *The Porcelain God: A Social History of the Toilet.* Secaucus, NJ: Birch Lane Press, 1996.

Ierley, Merritt. "The Bathroom: An Epic," *American Heritage*, 50:3 (May/Jun 1999): 76ff.

Inglis, David. *A Sociological History of Excretory Experience.* Lewiston, NY: Edwin Mellin Press, 2000.

Kelley, Victoria. *Soap and Water: Cleanliness, Dirt, and the Working Classes in Victorian and Edwardian Britain.* London and New York: I. B. Tauris, 2010.

Laporte, Dominique (Rodolphe el-Khoury and Nadia Benabid, trans.). *History of Shit.* Cambridge, MA: MIT Press, 2000.

Monestier, Martin. *Histoire et Bizarreries Sociales des Excréments.* Paris: Cherche Midi, 1997.

Muir, Frank. *An Irreverent & Almost Complete Social History of the Bathroom*. London: Heinemann, 1982.

Needham, Joseph, and Tsuen-Hsuin, Tsien. *Science and Civilization in China*, Volume 5: Chemistry and Chemical Technology: Part I: Paper and Printing. Cambridge, Eng.: Cambridge University Press, 1985.

Persels, Jeff, ed. *Fecal Matters in Early Modern Literature and Art*. Burlington, VT: Ashgate Pub., 2004.

Picard, Lisa. Elizabeth's London: *Everyday Life in Elizabethan London*. New York: St. Martin's Press, 2004.

Reynolds, Reginald. *Cleanliness and Godliness*. London, George Allen & Unwin, 1943.

Sabbath, Dan. *End Product: The First Taboo*. New York : Urizen Books, 1977.

Scobie, Alex. "Slums, Sanitation & Mortality in the Roman World," *Klio* 68:2 (1986): 399-433.

Saint-Simon, Duc de (Desmond Flower, selection/editor/translator). *The Memoirs of Louis de Rouvroy, Duc de Saint-Simon Covering the Years 1691-1723.* New York: Limited Editions Club, 1959.

Scott Paper Company. *Annual Reports,* 1951-1980. Chester, PA: Scott Paper Company.

Smith, Virginia. *Clean: A History of Personal Hygiene and Purity.* New York: Oxford University Press, 2007.

Spector, Robert. *Shared Values, A History of Kimberly-Clark.* Lyme CT: Greenwich Publishing, 1997.

Spinrad, Paul. *Guide to Bodily Fluids.* San Francisco, CA: RE/Search Publications, 1994.

Tomes, Nancy. *The Gospel of Germs: Men, Women, and the Microbe in American Life.* Cambridge, MA: Harvard University Press, 1998.

Williams, Marilyn T. *Washing the Great Unwashed: Public Baths in Urban America, 1840-1920.* Columbus OH: Ohio State University Press, 1991.

Wright, Lawrence. Clean and Decent: *The Fascinating History of the Bathroom.* New York: Viking Press, 1960.

FOOTNOTES

[1] Laporte, p 10
[2] This expression originated with Elias Boudinot, Federalist delegate from New Jersey.
[3] Muir p146
[4] The Great Toilet Paper Cover Up, Canadian Business. Toronto: May 1978. Vol. 51, Iss. 5; pg. 46
[5] Wiping appears in only two Hollywood movies that I know of: Jane Fonda wipes herself in *Fun With Dick and Jane* (1977) and Melanie Griffith does the same in *Something Wild* (1986)
[6] Henderson, p. 187
[7] see Gatrell, Vic, *City of Laughter* (New York: Walker & Co., 2006)
[8] Bourke, p.44
[9] http://www.museomadre.it/opere.cfm?id=55&evento=15
[10] Freud, S., foreword to: Bourke, John, *The Portable Scatalog* (New York: William Morrow, 1994) p.7
[11] Nouvelles Lettres de M. la Duchesse d'Orleans, Paris 1853 p332-135
[12] 'Factors associated with intestinal parasitic infection among school children in a rural area of Kathmandu Valley, Nepal', Nepal Medical College Journal, Jun 2005; Vol. 7, pp. 43-6
[13] Josephus, *History of the Jews*, book 2, chapter 8
[14] Quoted in Smith, p. 139
[15] Al-Sheikh, Abdul Fattah, *Water and Sanitation in Islam*, WHO pamphlet, 1996
[16] Aytac Sıdıka Mine, The Social and Technical Development of Toilet Design, (Izmir, Turkey: Izmir Institute of Technology 2004)
[17] Smith p.170
[18] Cohen, p. 221
[19] Blount, *Voyage into the Levant*, London (1634)
[20] Gatrell p.66
[21] Williams, p. 1
[22] George, p.174
[23] Clarke, John R., Look Who's Laughing: Humor In Tavern Painting, *Memoirs of the American Academy in Rome* Vol. 43/44, (1998/1999), pp. 27-48
[24] Pecard, p. 144
[25] Quoted in Inglis, p. 166.
[26] Ibid, p. 169

[27] Monestier, p. 147
[28] Ierley, M., Epic of the Bathroom, *American Heritage*; May/Jun 1999, p. 76
[29] Hector Gavin quoted in Eveleigh, p 13
[30] Readers interested in exploring this topic should refer to Bouchet, Françoise *Parasite Remains in Archaeological Sites*. Mem Inst Oswaldo Cruz, Rio de Janeiro, Vol. 98(Suppl. I): 47-52, 2003
[31] Horan p.20
[32] Stephen, Ernest, *Oceania,* Vol. 7, No. 1 (Sep., 1936), p. 52
[33] *Tissue World*, November 2009
[34] http://www.scielo.br/pdf/mioc/v98s1/v98s1a19.pdf
[35] Thanissaro Bhikkhu ed., Vatta Khandhaka: Collection of Duties *A rulebook for Buddhist monks, The Vinaya Pitaka*
[36] Ibid
[37] Letter 70
[38] Poem 23
[39] Josephus, History of the Jews, book 2, chapter 9
[40] Hadith, Volume 1, Book 4, Number 157-60
[41] Al-Husseini, Abdul Fattah, *Water and Sanitation in Islam*
[42] http://www.islamic-laws.com/taharatandnajasat.htm
[43] ibid, paragraph two.
[44] Monestier, p 58 author's translation.
[45] Sabbath, Dan & Mandel Hall, *End product: the first taboo,* p. 208
[46] Muir, p 79
[47] Author's translation.
[48] As quoted in Needham, Joseph *Science and Civilization in China* vol 5 p.123
[49] Ibid.
[50] Inglis, p. 101
[51] John Balein his preface to John Leland's *The Laboryouse Journey*, 1589
[52] Monestier p. 60. Author's translation.
[53] CT Research Publications, The Eighteenth Century ; reel 2206, no. 7
[54] www.kosherimage.com/sbt.html
[55] Some of these facts are detailed in a 1904 British Court case *(Colley's Patents, Ld.* v. *British Patent Perforated Paper Company,* in Reports Of Patent, Design And Trade Mark Cases, Vol. XXI., No. 30, p.689
[56] http://caselaw.lp.findlaw.com/cgibin/getcase.pl?court=us&vol=152&invol=425

[57] Spector, p. 135
[58] Scott annual report for 1952
[59] See the Harvard Business School study of Scott Paper, Sept. 26, 1997.
[60] Kanner B. The soft sell. New York Magazine, 27 Sept. 1982:14-5
[61] You can watch the ads on their site: http://www.quilton.com.au/
[62] Hutchinson, R.I., Bacillary Dysentery, J Am Med Assoc. 1956;162(1):60-62
[63] http://www.nabt.org/websites/institution/File/pdfs/publications/abt/2006/068-07-0018.pdf
[64] Judah G, Donachie et al., in a study done for the Dept. of Infectious & Tropical Diseases, London School of Hygiene & Tropical Medicine
[65] Nepal Medical College Journal: 2005 Jun; Vol. 7 (1), pp. 43-6
[66] Reviews of Infectious Diseases, Vol. 10, NO. 1, Jan-Feb 1988, p. 218-222
[67] Han, A.M., Oo KN, Aye T., Personal toilet after defecation and the degree of hand contamination according to different methods used, Journal of Tropical Medical Hygiene, 1986 Oct; 89 (5) 237-41
[68] Birmingham ME, Lee LA, Ntakibirora, A household survey of dysentery in Burundi: implications for the current pandemic in sub-Saharan Africa. Bull. WHO 1997; 75(1): 45-53.
[69] The British Medical Journal, Vol. 2, No. 6143 (Oct. 7, 1978), p. 1024
[70] http://www.aeos.cn/En/Info/Html/2008-7/Info_6_15245519.html
[71] George, p. 61. This number, 57 sheet/person/day supplied by a representative of Charmin, may seem high but one must remember the TP is commonly used for many other purposes in addition to front and rear cleaning including: covering the toilet seat, taking off make-up, nose blowing and wiping the floor after that final drip.
[72] Spinrad, Paul, p. 12-13
[73] Horan, p.149
[74] Saint-Simon, Claude H., Memoirs of Louis XIV
[75] Saint Simon, ibid

Printed in Great Britain
by Amazon